Thinking About the World
Building Geography Foundations

Lawrence Brown

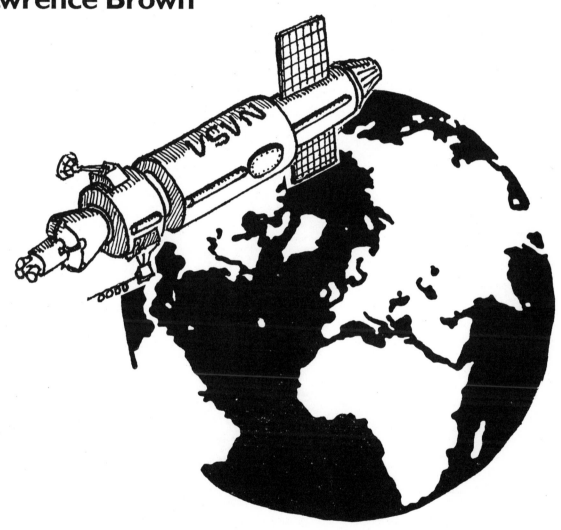

Addison-Wesley Publishing Company

Menlo Park, California • Reading, Massachusetts • New York
Don Mills, Ontario • Wokingham, England • Amsterdam • Bonn
Sydney • Singapore • Tokyo • Madrid • San Juan • Paris
Seoul, Korea • Milan • Mexico City • Taipei, Taiwan

Whitehouse

Managing Editor: Michael Kane
Project Editor: Mali Apple
Production: Karen Edmonds
Design: Detta Penna
Cover Art: David Woods

ISBN 0–201–45546–3

2 3 4 5 6 7 8 9 10-ML-96 95 94 93

Contents

To the Student

This book is a product of my experiences as a teacher and writer, and also as a parent. In all these capacities, I spend a lot of time explaining things to people, trying to make things clear, to show how things work and fit together. You might say I explain things for a living. Teachers—even the grumpy ones—wouldn't explain things for a living if they didn't love kids. We're half crazy as it is, but if we didn't love what we do and the people we do it for, we'd go completely crazy.

In 1986, my tiny geography class—Christine, Michael, Molly, Tahira, Gunnar, Becky, Amy, and Laura—couldn't stand their geography book, so they asked me to write one. You are holding the product of that request, and I thank them for insisting on it. Not many schools would let a teacher throw out a beautiful standard textbook and print his own instead. Mine did. Bright kids and inventive schools can do all kinds of useful things. I mention this to you because I think it's important for you not only to study hard, but also to think about how things are taught to you. If you get an idea about how you might learn something better, or have fun learning it, I hope you'll speak up and share ideas with your teachers—and I hope they will listen to you.

The key to any book is its language. I've decided to talk to you in the same voice I use with the kids in my classes. If a book can read like friendly and intelligent conversation, I hope you'll stay with it long enough to learn what you need to know. So I've written this imagining you were in the room with me, hearing my voice. I wish there were some way I could hear yours.

Geography is the study of the world and its people. Explaining it properly requires passion, patience, insight, irony, humor, tolerance, sympathy, rage, and wonder. These are things intelligent and sensitive people feel when thinking about the world. As teachers, we shouldn't tell you how to think and feel, but we can teach you in a way that you cannot help thinking and feeling a lot. It's not just a subject—it's your Earth we're talking about. The kind of life you will lead as adults depends on your understanding the Earth as completely as you can. I hope you'll care a lot.

Textbooks are filled with far more information than anyone can possibly remember beyond the next quiz. What if we want you to remember stuff *for life?* Then we have to ease up on the details and stress the basic concepts: what things mean . . . how things fit together. This needs more time, and the time must come from somewhere.

It is possible to discuss the world and its people without touching on controversies and without offending anyone. If we teach it that way, we'll offer you a boring fairyland, empty of the wisdom and passion citizens need. I hope you'll find a fascination with the issues that drive global history. You should be able to pick up a *Time* magazine (to *want* to pick up a *Time* magazine) and understand what's going on—and care. To do that, you must study the controversies that make the news. We can try mightily to be fair, but we can't look away. If we're not straight, we'll bore you to death and present you with a dishonest vision of a quiet Earth you already know isn't real.

Please remember you are reading the words of an individual. I have tried hard to be accurate and fair always. You should keep your eye on me—but then, you should keep your eye on *all* sources of opinion and information.

The world is a complex place. Although various experts have thought they'd found the secret ("It's all a matter of economics!" or whatever), if you're going to be thinking about the world, I suggest you keep as many factors in your head as possible: economics . . . religious faith . . . national pride . . . world view . . . lots of things. Simplify first to make sense of it all, but try not to fall into your own trap by believing the world is a simple place. It's not—but it can be understood. That's why I've written this book.

Lawrence W. Brown
Cape Cod Academy
Osterville, Mass.

Chapter 1

A Visitor from Space

Imagine looking at the Earth as a visitor from outer space might see it. (Better yet, imagine you are the Alien, seeing the Earth for the first time.) Imagine our celestial visitor coming down lower and lower.

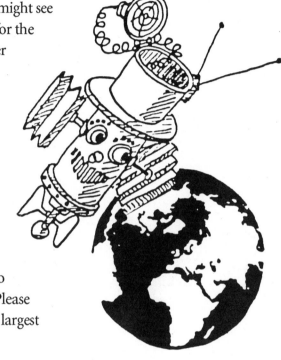

First off, our Alien would observe that the Earth is divided into oceans and landmasses. These would have to be explored and named. In fact, naming the various continents (large landmasses) and the oceans and seas (large bodies of salt water) is the first kind of work we need to do.

Our first map of Earth would show the continents, oceans, and seas. We can list the information on this map to make things easier to remember. Information is easier to remember when we "chunk" it into meaningful groups. (Please note, we have tried to simplify the maps by listing only the largest or most traveled features.)

Continents	**Oceans**	**Seas**
Africa	Pacific Ocean	North Sea
Antarctica	Atlantic Ocean	Baltic Sea
Asia	Indian Ocean	Mediterranean Sea
Australia	Arctic Ocean	Black Sea
Europe		Caspian Sea
North America		Red Sea
South America		Persian Gulf
		South China Sea
		Yellow Sea
		Sea of Japan
		Bering Sea
		Hudson Bay
		Gulf of Mexico
		Sea of Cortez
		Caribbean Sea

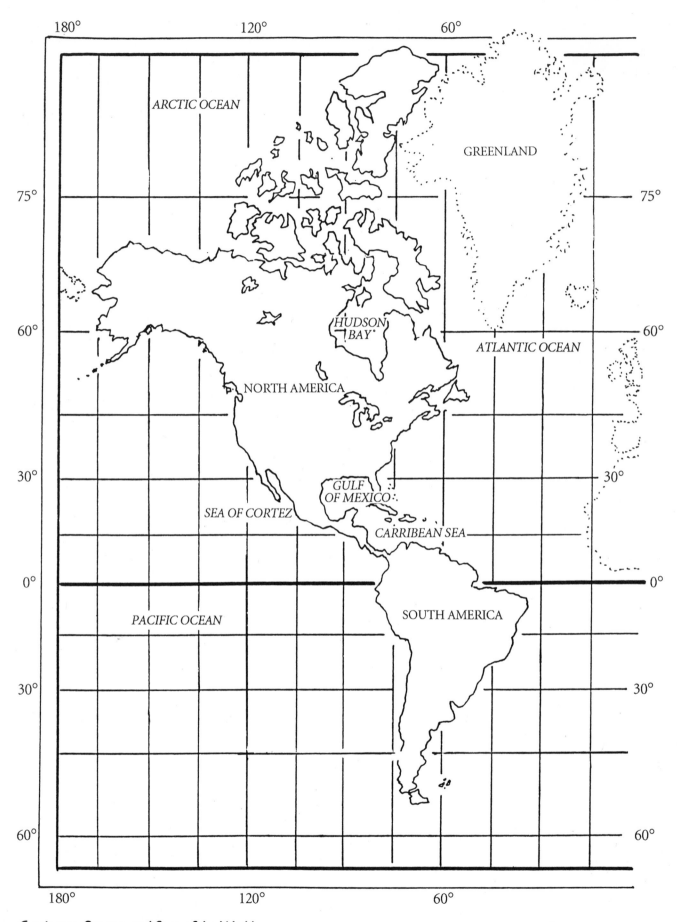

Continents, Oceans, and Seas of the World

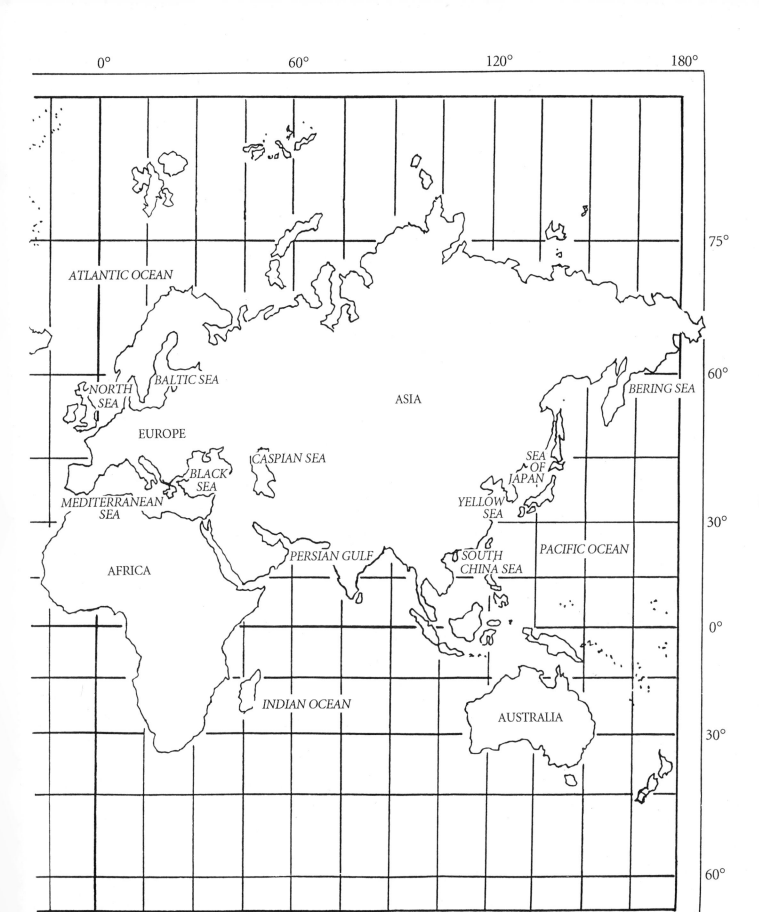

ATLANTIC OCEAN

75°

60°

BALTIC SEA

NORTH
SEA

BERING SEA

ASIA

EUROPE

CASPIAN SEA

SEA
OF
JAPAN

BLACK
SEA

YELLOW
SEA

MEDITERRANEAN
SEA

30°

PERSIAN GULF

SOUTH
CHINA SEA

PACIFIC OCEAN

AFRICA

0°

INDIAN OCEAN

AUSTRALIA

30°

60°

0°   60°   120°   180°

3

Flying still lower, our celestial visitor would soon notice a spectacular feature about our planet: mountain ranges. Knowing where these ranges are will help explain much about the rest of the Earth.

Our second map shows the major mountain ranges of the world. Here again, a list might be helpful.

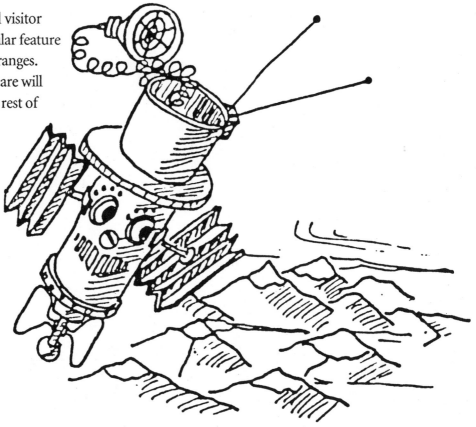

Africa
Atlas Mountains
Ethiopian Highlands
Cameroon Mountains
Drakensberg Mountains

North America
Appalachian Highlands
Rocky Mountains
Sierra Nevada/Cascade/Coastal/
   Alaska Range
Sierra Madre Mountains

Asia
Ural Mountains
Himalaya Mountains
Zagros Mountains

South America
Andes Mountains

Europe
Pyrenees
Alps
Caucasus Mountains
Balkans

180°   120°   60°

75°

60°

ALASKA
RANGE

COASTAL
RANGE

CASCADE
RANGE

SIERRA
NEVADA

ROCKY
MOUNTAINS

APPLACHIAN
HIGHLANDS

30°

SIERRA MADRE
MOUNTAINS

0°

30°

ANDES
MOUNTAINS

60°

75°

60°

30°

0°

30°

60°

180°   120°   60°

Major Mountain Ranges of the World

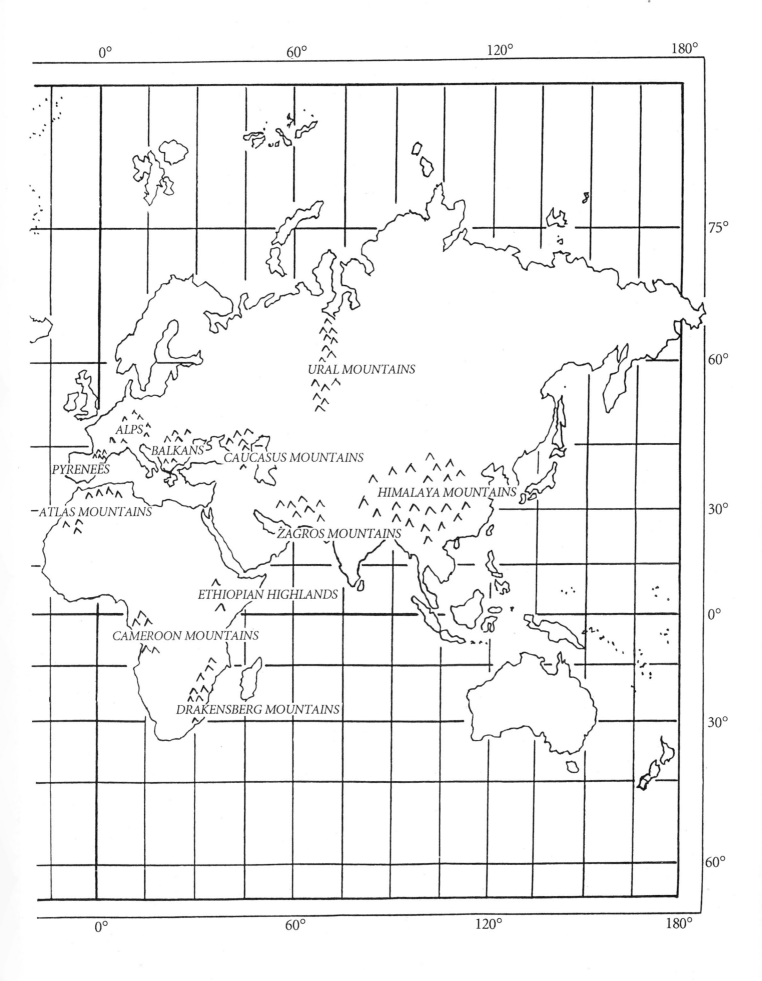

URAL MOUNTAINS

ALPS

BALKANS

CAUCASUS MOUNTAINS

PYRENEES

HIMALAYA MOUNTAINS

ATLAS MOUNTAINS

ZAGROS MOUNTAINS

ETHIOPIAN HIGHLANDS

CAMEROON MOUNTAINS

DRAKENSBERG MOUNTAINS

7

As our Alien gets nearer to the Earth, rivers appear. Water flows downhill, so wherever there are major mountain ranges (with snow on them that melts), you can expect rivers to flow out of them. It just makes sense. Also, clouds full of rain bump into the sides of high mountains and dump their moisture down the mountainsides—where the moisture finds its way into rivers.

Our third map shows the major rivers of the world, in most cases flowing down out of the major mountain ranges of the world. Here are the rivers, by continent. (Again, these are certainly not all of the rivers in the world, but the largest or most heavily used.)

Africa
Nile
Niger
Zaire (Congo)
Zambezi

Asia
Indus
Ganges
Brahmaputra
Mekong
Xi
Yangtze
Huang He (Yellow River)

Europe
Thames
Rhine
Seine
Loire
Rhone
Danube
Volga

North America
Saint Lawrence
Hudson
Delaware
Mississippi-Missouri-Ohio System
  *(includes Red, Platte, and
  Arkansas Rivers)*
Rio Grande
Colorado
Columbia
Fraser
Mackenzie

South America
Orinoco
Amazon
Rio de la Plata

Middle Eastern
Tigris
Euphrates
Shatt al Arab *(the river
  formed by the other two,
  after they join)*

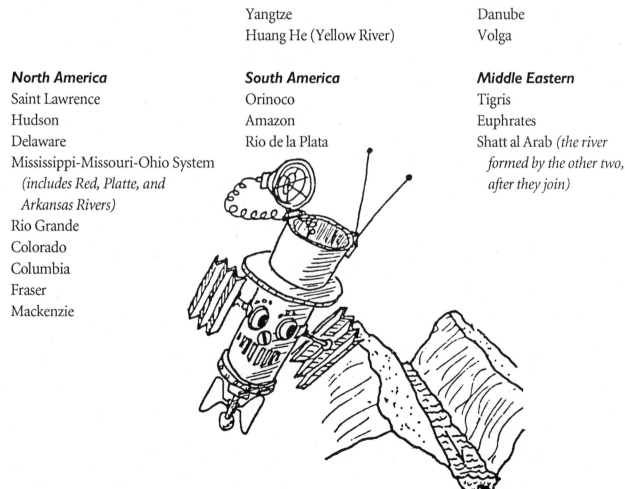

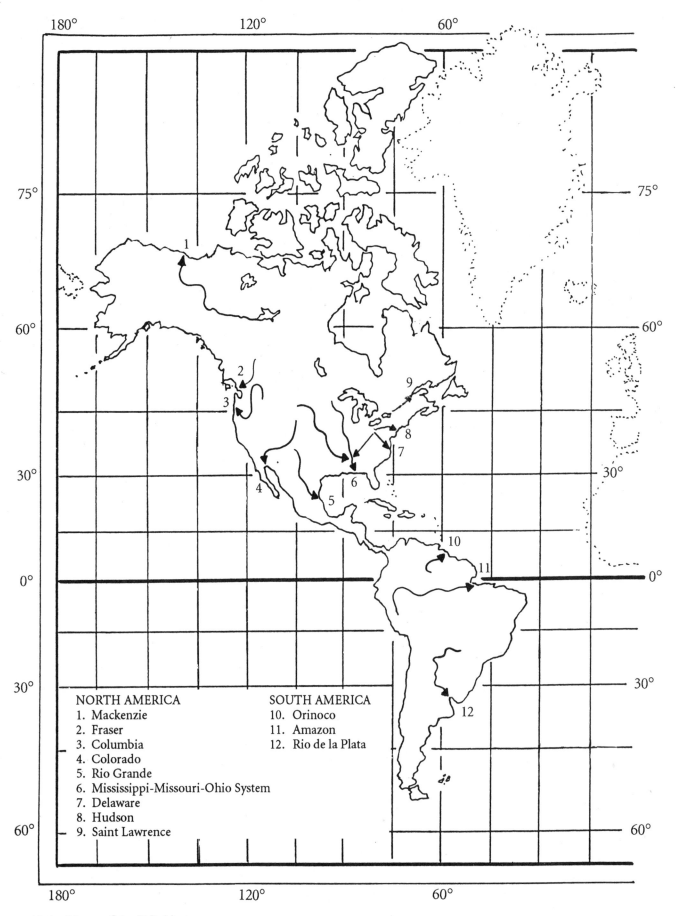

NORTH AMERICA
1. Mackenzie
2. Fraser
3. Columbia
4. Colorado
5. Rio Grande
6. Mississippi-Missouri-Ohio System
7. Delaware
8. Hudson
9. Saint Lawrence

SOUTH AMERICA
10. Orinoco
11. Amazon
12. Rio de la Plata

Major Rivers of the World

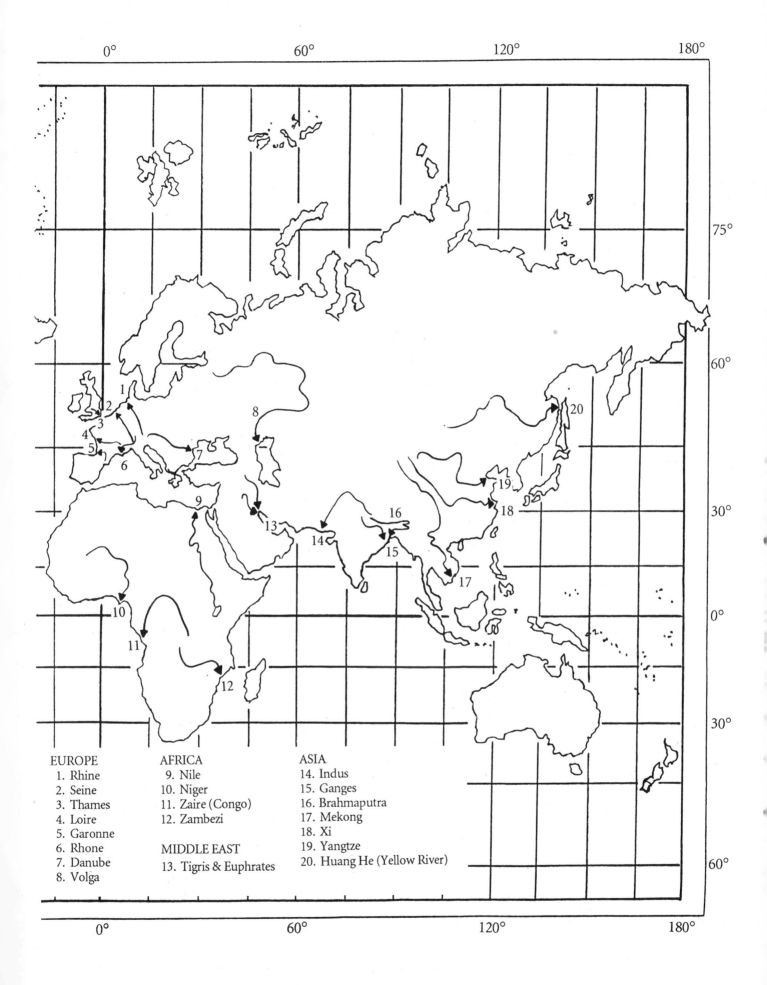

| 0° | 60° | 120° | 180° |

75°

60°

30°

0°

30°

60°

EUROPE
1. Rhine
2. Seine
3. Thames
4. Loire
5. Garonne
6. Rhone
7. Danube
8. Volga

AFRICA
9. Nile
10. Niger
11. Zaire (Congo)
12. Zambezi

MIDDLE EAST
13. Tigris & Euphrates

ASIA
14. Indus
15. Ganges
16. Brahmaputra
17. Mekong
18. Xi
19. Yangtze
20. Huang He (Yellow River)

| 0° | 60° | 120° | 180° |

Kinds of Climates

Our visitor continues to descend and becomes aware of climate. (It's hotter some places than others; it rains and snows more some places than others.) Being a compulsive organizer, our Alien zooms around the planet, then classifies the world's climates into groups.

Project 1   *Classifying Climates*

Pretend you're the Alien. How are you going to classify the climates of planet Earth? Maybe the class can organize ideas on the chalkboard.

- First, what kind of system would you use? What do we think of when we think of climate? What kinds of questions do you ask when you ask about the climate of a place (hot-cool . . . wet-dry . . . etc.)?

- Once you know how you're going to talk about it, how are you going to classify the climates of Earth? Devise a system of descriptive names for the various climate zones. Does the system cover the kinds of climates you know about? Have you left anything out?

- Now, compare your system of descriptive names with the one below. Does your system describe climates not covered by the terms below?

Arctic   In the far north and far south—at the top and bottom of the Earth—it is cold all year long. It can snow almost any time, and in the winter, temperatures can drop to 60 degrees Fahrenheit below zero, or more!

Alpine   As in the Swiss Alps (the mountains), you're high up in alpine areas. Summers are cool and refreshing; winters are cold and very snowy. (And remember, snow melting in the summers helps to fill the Earth's rivers.)

Maritime   These areas are near oceans and seas. Oceans are so large that they take a long time to warm in summer and to cool in winter—so they're always cooler than the summer air and warmer than the winter winds. The oceans moderate the climate, and make it damper, too. Places near oceans often have milder climates than places farther inland. Maritime climates often have more fog than the others, too.

Continental   In the interior of continents, oceans don't moderate climates at all. Winters are usually very cold; summers are very hot.

Desert   Like the arctic, this is a potentially deadly climate: always dry, and usually very hot.

Tropical   These areas are hot and wet. Sometimes tropical places have a rainy season, in which it rains almost daily, then a drier season. (Oddly, tropical rainforests are often sitting on desert sand. If the rainforests are cut or damaged, the sun bakes the ground, the moisture dries, and the desert returns.)

And now an important point: As a celestial visitor, you have decided on your descriptive names for climates. How else can you talk intelligently about this place to the folks back home?

Aliens and humans alike use descriptive names to make sense of the world and for conversation—but in reality, the world isn't as neatly organized as that. Changes from climate to climate are gradual. Places can be *semi-arctic* for example; between arctic and continental. It becomes especially important when we talk about people to remember that the Earth is a complicated and subtle place. *The Earth and its people are real; the terms we use to describe them are just for our conversation.* Sometimes people forget that and make their words more important to them than the realities they describe. They talk about climates and economies and races and religions as if there were neat little boxes into which everything fits. We have to keep remembering it's not like that, really. Language sometimes gets us into trouble.

The next map shows the Earth divided into climate zones.

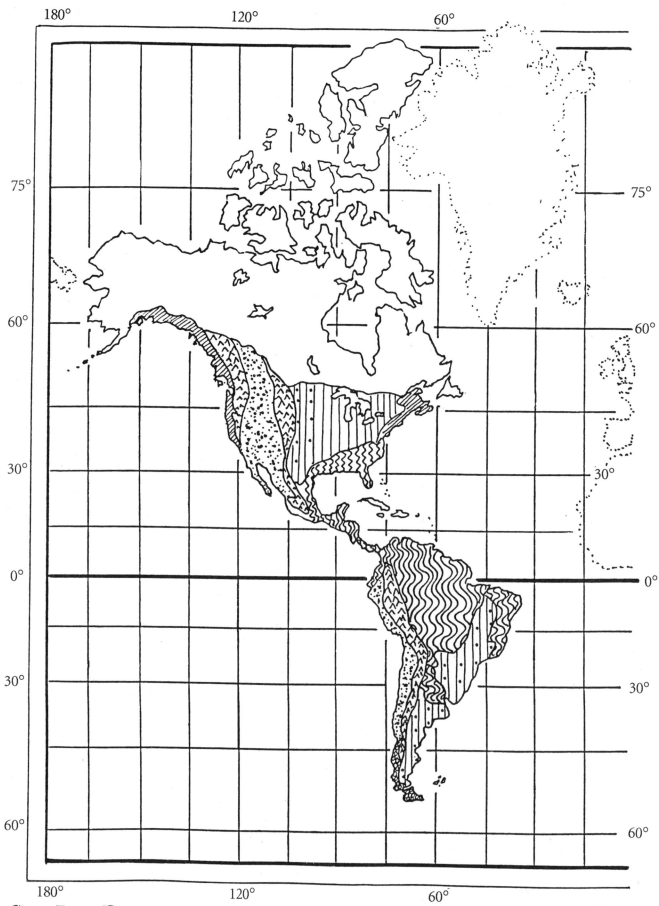

Climate Zones of the World

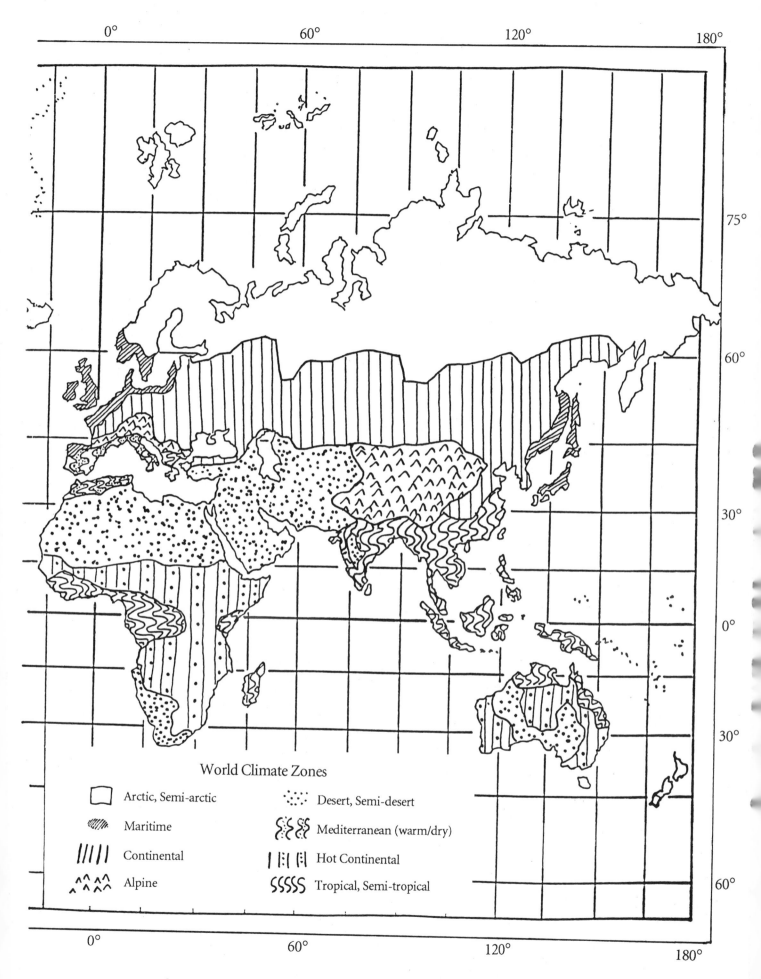

World Climate Zones

☐	Arctic, Semi-arctic	∴	Desert, Semi-desert
▨	Maritime	ऽऽऽ	Mediterranean (warm/dry)
‖‖‖	Continental	⦙⦙⦙	Hot Continental
∧∧∧	Alpine	SSSS	Tropical, Semi-tropical

When you begin to learn about the nations and peoples of the Earth, it makes sense to follow the approach of our extraterrestrial visitor.

We will come down from a great height, naming the major landmasses and bodies of water first. Then, we'll look for mountains and any large rivers that might be flowing out of them. Next, we'll see what kinds of climates the place has. We'll be curious to see what kinds of people are living on the land: where they came from, what languages they speak, what customs they have, how the men and the women treat each other and what they expect from each other, and how they treat people from other places and what they expect of strangers.

Then we will look at three more big subjects: economics, politics, and religion. We can't think intelligently about the world until we know these basic things about countries and their peoples.

Continents, oceans, and seas . . . mountain ranges . . . major rivers . . . climates . . . peoples. . . the ways countries make a living . . . economic systems . . . forms of government . . . religious beliefs . . . that's our system.

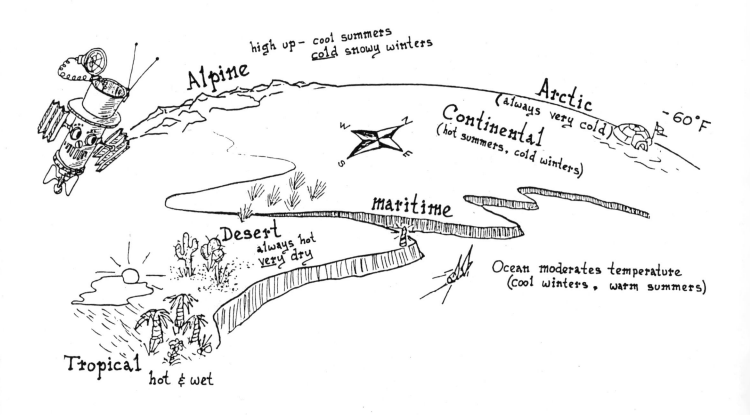

Chapter 2

Drawing Maps of Your Own

Now don't get nervous. So your maps won't look like Rand McNally maps on your first time out. Who cares? Everyone can draw maps, and in doing it, you learn how things look in a way that stays with you. There are a number of approaches to this; let's look at several.

Project 2 *Drawing Maps from Personal Experience*

Here's a good project to do in pairs. When your maps are finished, exchange them with your partner. Have your partner "talk you through" the map you've drawn to see whether you've been clear. ("Let's see now. If I've got you right, I drive south on Elm Street and turn left at the gas station. . . .")

♦ Here's an easy one: Draw a map showing how your bedroom is laid out—where the beds, tables, and so on, are. Socks and trash on the floor are optional. For mapmakers, such things are matters of scale or detailing.

♦ Now, draw a map showing your partner how to get from your bedroom to the bathroom.

♦ Now, draw a map showing your partner how to get from your home to school. Forget artistry; accuracy is key. Can your partner follow your map step by step and actually end up at the school? This is the first basic kind of map—something drawn from personal experience designed to tell someone else how to find something without dragging you along the whole route as a guide.

♦ Now, hide something and then give people a map showing them how to find it. Pirates used to do this. This can be a whole activity in itself, using the school and its grounds in which to hide things. Candy kisses make good "treasures" to hide.

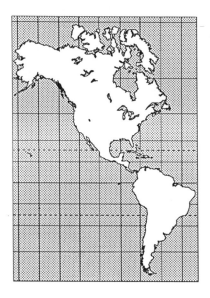

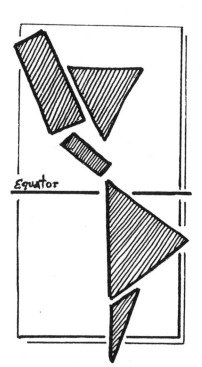

Equator

Project 3   *Simplifying Maps for Basic Information*

Look at the American continent on a map. It's complicated, isn't it? How could you possibly remember how to draw it perfectly? Still, you could learn how to at least draw the basic shapes of the continents.

First there's the matter of *proportion* (how big some things are compared to other things) and *location* (where things are in relation to other things). Notice, for example, that South America is not only south of North America, it's to the right of it! Mexico and Central America run southeast in a long slant. On a finished map, you should be able to look south from Florida and trace the west coast of South America.

Maybe it would help sometimes to break up a complicated figure into a bunch of simple shapes. Artists do this all the time. This approach does not give you all of the details, but that's fine.

♦ Try making maps of this sort with Africa . . . with Australia. Now a hard one: try making a map of the Middle East with East Africa, the Red Sea, the Persian Gulf, and the land all the way to India.

♦ You can have a contest with this. As a class, choose one continental subject, say Africa. As homework, all of you can devise ways to simplify and draw its shape. Then in class, each of you draws your solution on the chalkboard from memory. The most accurate or most creative solution wins.

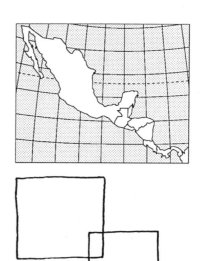

Project 4 · *Freehand Drawing Central America*

Even fairly complicated places can be drawn with some practice. I'll bet there are lots of people in the State Department who can't draw Central America—but you can! Freehand drawing your own maps is the best way there is to learn where things are in the world and how the pieces and places fit together.

♦ First, try Central America. Start simply with the basic proportions, then work from there. Use the corners of the boxes as reference points. Learn what goes in first one box, then the other. The only way you can do this is to practice it over and over. See how the Baja Peninsula hangs down off the left side of the upper box? The Yucatan peninsula fits into the place where the boxes overlap—and remember the single big hump in the middle of the lower box. This system bends Panama around a bit, but that's okay.

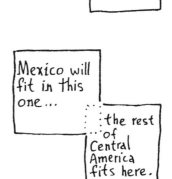

You can even put in the countries. Again, the detailing is left out, but you learn how everything fits together this way. Find little Belize in the bottom right-hand corner where the boxes overlap. From the upper-left corner of Belize, lines go out and down to form the edges of Guatemala. A diagonal line through the hump in the lower box divides Honduras and Nicaragua.

♦ Try this approach with other regions of the globe. As homework, try searching the world map for likely places to try this approach. Bring to class the places you find.

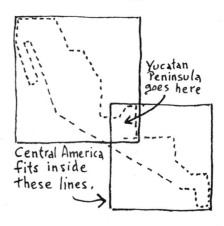

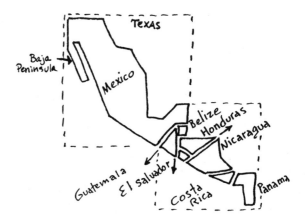

19

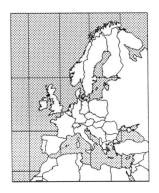

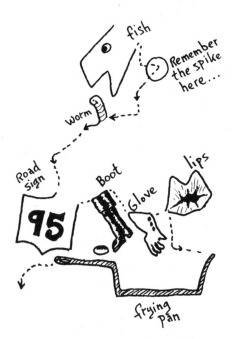

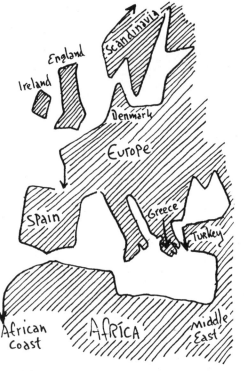

Many years ago, people had no television. They passed the time on mild nights laying in the grass on their backs looking up at the stars. (It's still a neat thing to do.) Sometimes, they tried to imagine that the stars formed patterns of recognizable things: bears . . . big spoons . . . mythical gods . . . archers, and so on. We can remember the shape of Europe in just this way—by associating physical features of Europe with the shapes of things we know.

♦ Look at the illustration and you'll get the idea. Remember what features are to the north, to the south, or on the same line as other features. Then practice until you get it right. As always, you won't really know a place until you can draw it from memory. The details may not be perfect, but you'll have a useful picture in your mind, and that's good enough.

♦ This approach is like imagining geographical constellations. Try it with another difficult zone: Southeast Asia. See what images you come up with, and share them with the class on the chalkboard, or with a partner.

Project 6   *Drawing the Globe on a Balloon*

Here's a project that pulls all of your skills together. Imagine yourself in the court of King Ferdinand and Queen Isabella of Spain. You have appeared there by magic in your jeans and T-shirt. They are astonished. It's 1491, and they're trying to figure out what to make of this Columbus fellow: he claims he will find a shorter route to the Indies by sailing west. "He's got it all wrong!" you shout. "Look; it's like *this* really." You whip out a balloon, blow it up, and begin to draw in the outlines of the continents with a marker. On go the equator and four meridians . . . the "Old" World and then *the "New" World!* Imagine the excitement. You would probably end up being burned alive. Christopher Columbus would make four voyages to the Americas and be brought home in chains. Who said history was going to be fair?

If you can draw the globe on a balloon, you'll know more geography than at least 95 percent of your fellow citizens— and far more than most anyone your age. Of course if everybody had to learn how to do this. . . .

Here's how you do it. Obviously, you want a round balloon, not a hotdog-shaped one. A light-colored balloon works best. Don't blow it up too big or it might burst while you're drawing. A ballpoint pen writes well on balloons, but is risky. An indelible marker is best. (If you like, first practice parts of this on flat sheets of paper.)

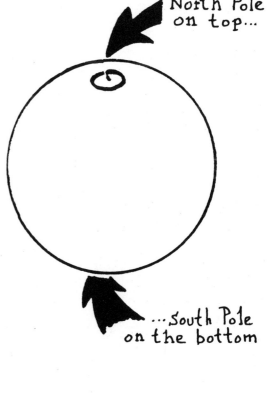

North Pole on top...

...South Pole on the bottom

♦ Draw the North Pole on top and an irregular circle on the bottom for Antarctica.

♦ Draw the Equator around the globe's middle.

♦ From the North Pole, draw four lines of longitude all the way to the South Pole. These four lines of longitude—which are also two circles called *meridians* that pass through the poles—divide the globe into four sections. Use your meridians to space and locate things.

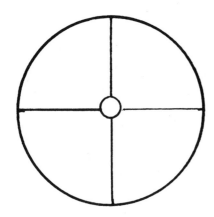

♦ From the top and bottom, your balloon should look like this.

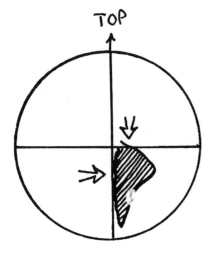

♦ Draw in South America just south of the Equator and to the right of one of the meridians. We'll use the Equator and the same meridian to locate North America.

♦ Draw in North America just north of the Equator and to the left of the meridian. Central America slants downward to connect North and South America.

♦ Now, move to the other side of the globe by following the meridian around. (It's just to the north of the Equator.)

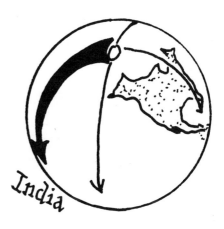

♦ Now you're looking on the opposite side from North and South America. Draw a V to locate India. Africa will be to the left of it. Asia will be to the right of it.

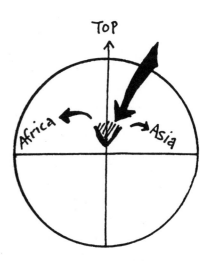

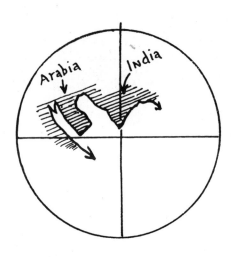

♦ From India, go west (to the left) and draw in the Persian Gulf . . . come out and around Arabia . . . and draw the Red Sea.

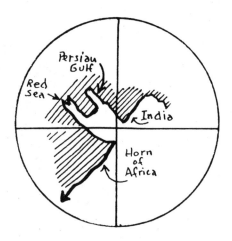

♦ Now draw what's called "the Horn" of Africa, and then stop. (Look at this area on an atlas and you'll see why it is called the Horn. It resembles a bull's horn—sort of.)

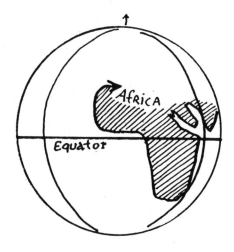

♦ Rotate the globe a bit to the right. India is on your right-hand side. Now, draw the rest of Africa's coastline. Note that the Atlantic bulge of Africa is north of the Equator.

♦ Now you have to take a big breath and draw in the outline of Europe. Start with the top of the Mediterranean Sea: Spain (resembles a stop sign) . . . Italy (boot) . . . Greece (glove). Add the Black Sea (lips) north of Turkey, and don't forget the Caspian Sea off to the right. Up you go along the coast of France. Do Denmark and Scandinavia (worm and fish).

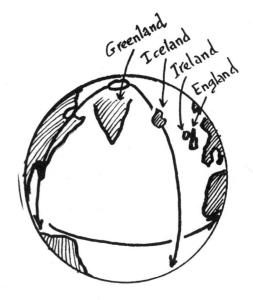

♦ Remember that Greenland is up there between Canada and Europe. Don't forget Iceland . . . and draw in England and Ireland off the coast of France.

♦ Back to India! Now go to the right. The Malay Peninsula pokes down south of the Equator a bit . . . draw a little bulge for Southeast Asia and a bigger one for China . . . draw in Korea, then run a long squiggly line all the way along the top of Asia and Europe and back to Scandinavia . . . add the island groups of Japan, Taiwan, and the Philippines. They're off the coast of China and Korea.

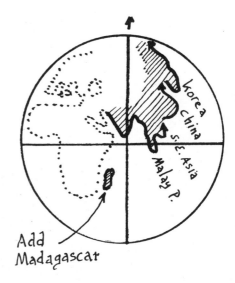

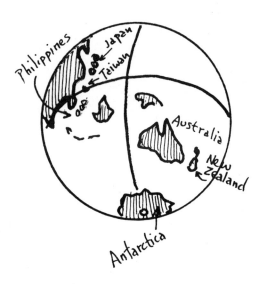

♦ Now draw in Australia, New Zealand, and the Pacific island groups as best you can.

And you've done it! You can paint your finished globes with acrylic colors . . . create a display in your classroom . . . even hang them from the ceiling.

Chapter 3

The Ethnic Earth

Our celestial visitor finally comes close enough to discover the human beings swarming all over the planet. Clearly, these beings are all of the same kind, yet in coloring and in other details, they also have their differences. On our visitor's planet, racial differences have nothing to do with color. How will these beings be described in the official reports? The Alien notes that, in general, in the hottest places, people appear the darkest. The peoples of Africa seem to be a group to our Alien, as do the peoples of Asia and Europe. Had he come earlier, our Alien would have seen millions of Native Americans—the only Americans at one time—but so many were killed that they escape his notice completely.

Naturally, human beings come in all shapes, colors, and sizes, but our Alien struggles to devise a system of some sort, as with the climates, to describe and categorize the creatures.

Project 7 *Organizing Humanity*

Stop reading! You must promise to stop right here and read no further until you've played a mind game. You're the Alien again, trying to make sense of things. How can you understand the enormous variety of human beings?

Human beings organize themselves in all sorts of ways, but assume for the moment *the only things you know about the Earth's people are the things you can observe for yourself.* You can look at the human beings themselves, their bodies and the clothes they wear . . . you can listen to them converse . . . you can observe their behavior and see how they live. But you can't read their minds and know about their ideas yet. So if you were going to organize humanity into groups or categories, how would you do it?

♦ This project can be done with your whole class. Use the chalkboard to organize class thoughts. As you look at human beings through the eyes of the Alien, what differences do you see? How would you organize human beings based on those differences? Resolve disagreements with a vote. This can be interesting: humanity often puts its neighbors into groups with anger or prejudice in its heart—as an organized system of insults or name-calling. As a visitor from outer space, you have no prejudices at all. You just want to organize what you're looking at in some meaningful way so you can explain this place to the folks back home. What will you come up with?

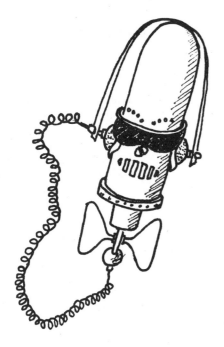

Then the Alien tunes in to Earthling radio . . .

Now something wonderful happens! Our space visitor discovers human electronic transmissions and begins listening in on our radios. Once it's clear that the electronic babble is language—in fact, many languages—our Alien starts to learn a lot. Human beings, like our Alien, are also engaged in the confusing process of trying to categorize one another with systems of descriptive names. Clearly, languages are still another way these people separate themselves from one another. As the languages are decoded, the Alien begins to connect languages and places: people from one place often speak the same language. So where people come from (or once came from) is another way of classifying human beings.

Soon our celestial visitor begins to notice still another kind of difference between human beings. It's first noticed in the few places left where people wear little or no clothing: human beings seem to come in two basic types. Our Alien is tempted to think of these as gender—sex—differences, but since there are twelve genders on the Alien's home planet, it's hard for our visitor to imagine only two. It makes our visitor a little sad to think of how dull it must be—but maybe with more information, everything would be clearer.

After some fooling around with the dials, the Alien starts picking up television transmissions too. This is like being on the planet's surface without being seen! The Alien becomes more convinced than ever that there are genders on Earth, and that things are not as dull as they first appeared. Humans seem to have all kinds of ideas about what to expect from people of different sexes, colors, and speech . . . and it seems almost any sort of difference is reason enough for Earthlings to act unkindly.

Then, there is the more complicated issue of religious faith. *Religion* is the belief in some kind of supernatural presence and the attempt to establish a relationship with it.

Here we have one of the two principal points of difference in the world's religions: *one god or many?* What we call in modern times the Western religions (Judaism, Christianity, and Islam) agree there is only one God. The major Eastern religions (Hinduism and Buddhism) believe with equal certainty there are many gods.

The other principal point of difference in the world's religions is this: *one life or many?* Does our soul have only one time on Earth (the belief of Western religions), or does it return to the flesh again and again (the belief of Eastern religions)? Do we learn what must be learned in one life and then face the judgement of God (Western religions), or do we learn life's lessons more gradually and escape this life to join the Divine only when we have learned them all (Eastern religions)? Whereas the Western religions see life on Earth as the battleground where each soul struggles between good and evil, the Eastern religions see life on Earth as a spider's web from which each soul struggles to be free.

The world's religions differ on many issues, but these are the big ones. The religious traditions of the world have left a richer legacy of thought and inspiration than any human being could possibly absorb in a lifetime of study. There is, in every major faith, a vision of how the world might be if the lives of people were transformed by love and belief.

Thinking About Ethnicity

The Alien notes in a log the human language for discussing differences between people.

Ethnic   Used to describe the whole study of where people come from and their varied dress and customs.

Linguist *or* **language**   Refers to the different systems of sounds (and often gestures) different groups of people use to communicate with one another.

Race   Refers to the apparent differences between people based on skin color and other physical details.

Gender   Refers to the differences between sexes, the roles and expectations each have for the other, and the ways they treat each other.

Religion   Covers all of the ways people understand the supernatural, their beliefs in God (or gods), and their ways of seeking a relationship with the Divine.

From the radio and television transmissions, our Alien learns that these are the basic ways human beings separate themselves into groups. (There are other ways, too. They come later.) This is enough to puzzle the Alien. Clearly, human beings are far better at separating themselves from one another than they are at getting together. The Alien imagines that this skill of seeing differences between people must have been important to humanity at some time in the distant past, because the skills are so highly developed everywhere and practiced so continually. The Alien wonders what possible use these skills could have been.

Project 8   *Tracing the Languages of North America*

One measure of how completely the Native American cultures were destroyed is that we don't even know how many people were living in the Americas before the arrival of Columbus. We believe there may have been around 24 million Aztecs in what is now Mexico when Hernando Cortés arrived in 1519. (That's not quite the population of present-day Canada.) Within a generation, the native population dropped to less than a tenth of that. It was to be much the same throughout most of North and South America. Then, as Europeans settled the land in greater numbers, native populations fell even more drastically.

What happened? First of all, there was warfare between the new arrivals and those already living in the Americas. Possessing firearms, the Europeans had an extraordinary advantage. Even more destructive in the long run were European diseases, against which the native populations had no resistance. Whole peoples and ways of living vanished—often before the new settlers had the time or interest to even record what was being lost.

♦ How can we see this process graphically? With a map, we can get a clear view. We could use two maps to record a picture of the Americas before Columbus and after—but maybe using a single map would be the most dramatic. After all, there was only one land. So what we'll do is give you a picture of the land as it was ten seconds before Columbus's longboat first dug its nose into the Caribbean sand.

On this map, we'll put some (though certainly not all) of the Native American peoples who lived here. Then *right on top* of their locations (because that's how it happened) you can locate the Europeans. The simplest way to organize the European populations is by language. We'll give each language group a graphic code, and you'll cover the map occupied by each group with its own graphic.

So for *the Americas as they are today,* we'll cover the continents like this:

 Areas where Spanish-speaking people live.

 Areas where English-speaking people live.

 Areas where French-speaking people live.

 Areas where Native-American languages are the principal languages used.

Where can you find this information? Look for a world atlas in your library or classroom, or look in an encyclopedia under the entry *language.*

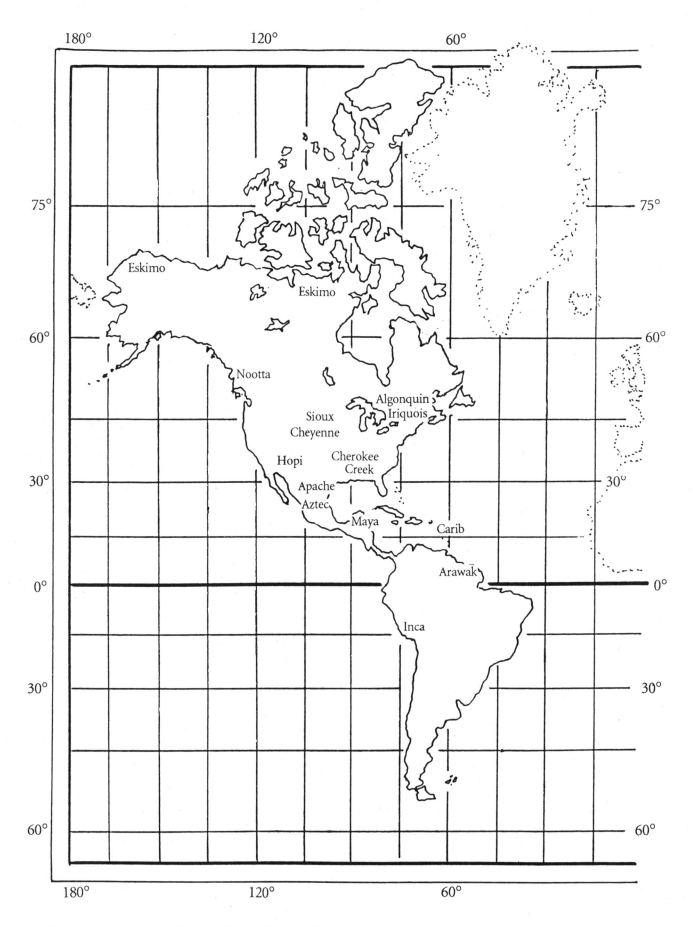

180° 120° 60°

75° 75°

Eskimo

Eskimo

60° 60°

Nootta

Algonquin
Iriquois

Sioux
Cheyenne

Hopi Cherokee
Creek

Apache 30°
30° Aztec

Maya Carib

Arawak

0° 0°

Inca

30° 30°

60° 60°

180° 120° 60°

Some Native American Peoples Before Columbus's Landing

Chapter 4

The Economic Earth

On the Earth, everything must eat to live. For human beings, this process is most complicated. We refer to this business as "making a living". . . everybody has to do it somehow. Whole *countries* (and parts of countries) do things to make a living too, and what they do is often determined by the geography of the place. For example:

International trade   As we look down from our flying saucer, we see a land with a mighty river flowing through it. Deep rivers are usually ideal for large ships to pass up and down. Luckily for this country, this large river has a sheltered harbor at its mouth, protected from ocean storms by a peninsula (a finger of land sticking out into the water). Ships from around the world can come here to bring goods to sell and load up with stuff to take back home. In developed countries, you'll find *international trading* cities near the mouth of most major rivers. These places are where the nations of the world do business with each other.

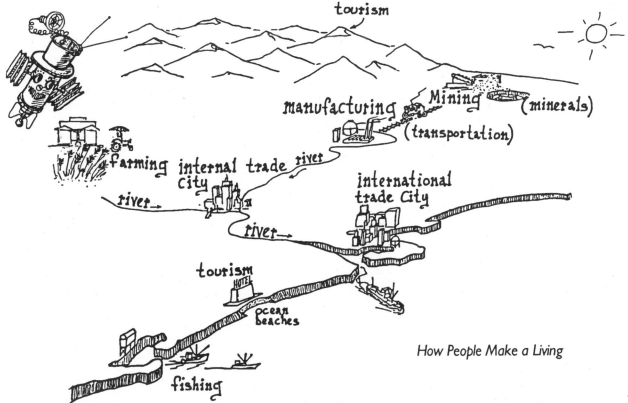

How People Make a Living

Internal trade   If we follow these deep rivers back into the interior until it's too shallow for a ship to pass, we'll usually find *internal trading* cities—especially where two rivers join. These are ideal spots for the people within a country to do business with each other, since it's easy to float goods around on barges and ships. Places where railroad lines and highways join make good internal trading locations too and, as nations grow, what were once convenient riverside loading points grow slowly into major population centers.

Food production   Here's another way countries make a living. They grow food, catch fish, and raise livestock for meat (and obtain wool and hides for leather). Poor countries that can't afford factories for industry can still make money farming.

Mining   The process of getting valuable substances out of the ground. For simplicity, we'll include oil and natural gas in the list of valuable things we find in the earth. There are all kinds of metals, gold, silver, iron, and aluminum—as well as useful minerals and chemicals.

Manufacturing   The making of *finished products* out of *raw materials* such as wood, iron, and chemicals. Manufacturing also refers to the making of the basic materials out of which complicated things are produced: smelting iron into steel to make automobiles . . . blowing and pressing glass to make light bulbs and windows . . . making plastics out of petroleum (oil) and other chemicals . . . and making machines that can be used to make other things.

We call the manufacturing of clothing (textiles) and electronics *light industry. Heavy industry* refers to manufacturing of steel and iron products, especially jobs that require a lot of energy.

Service   Doing things for others that don't require the actual manufacturing of anything: for example, some service jobs involve teaching, healing, communications, information ser-vices, sanitation, cooking, or solving problems. These jobs often aren't glamorous, but they are the glue that holds countries and their economies together.

Tourism   In certain places, a major source of income. Some nations without either industry or large farms have mountains or nice beaches. They depend on tourism to bring in needed money.

Transportation The moving of people and products from place to place. Developed countries depend heavily on transportation. (In the United States, food products travel, on the average, over a thousand miles from the farm to your dinner table.)

Prosperous countries have all of these ingredients in place and can make money all eight ways. What we call *developing* countries lack, for one reason or another, whole pieces of the puzzle. Of course, the economies of nations are more complex than this. Still, this is a good way to begin thinking about a complicated subject: economics.

Thinking About Economics

Economics is the study of how money is made and distributed. Economics is a complicated subject, but it can be understood by ordinary people. Anyone who has to earn a wage and survive in the world (in other words, almost everybody) deserves to know something about how money is made in the world and who gets to have it and how much. Ignorance can be far more expensive than a new car.

To discuss economics intelligently, we'll need a vocabulary. Here are some terms used to describe the places where people live and work.

Urban   A densely populated area . . . in the city.

Suburban *(sub-urban)*   A fairly populated area, but not too crowded . . . near the city, but not *in* it.

Rural *(or exurban)*   A thinly populated area . . . in the country.

Here are some terms to discuss business dealings and the trade between countries.

Goods   Merchandise . . . things to be sold.

Market   A place where goods can be sold. (A whole country can be a market for another country's goods.)

Monopoly   A situation in which only one or a few people have the opportunity to buy or sell goods.

Please learn this before continuing.

Raw materials   The basic materials out of which *finished goods* or *manufactured goods* are made, such as wood, rubber, and iron.

Import   To bring goods into one country from another country. When you buy goods from other countries, their product comes in, your money goes out (to them).

Export   To send goods out of one country so that people from other lands can buy them. (Your goods go out; someone else's money comes in.)

Balance of trade   The difference between how much of its products a country sells to other nations and how much it buys from other nations. If a nation buys more than it sells, *it's losing money.* Nations want a "favorable" balance of trade.

Invest   To put money in a bank or business with the hope of making more money with it. You don't invest in a candy bar (something you eat), but you might invest in a stock or a savings bond.

Capital   Money one has to invest in a bank or in a business. A *capitalist* is someone who has or uses capital.

Profit   What capitalists hope to make. If you invest in a business and you make more money than doing business costs you, the surplus money you cleared is profit.
Earnings – Expenses = Profit.

What's a Dollar Worth?

Money is funny stuff. You'd think it would be easy to answer the question, "What's a dollar worth?" but it's not. We can learn something about economics by *trying* to answer the question, though. There are at least two ways people have tried to answer this question.

The first way: "A dollar is worth what stands behind it." Here is a paper dollar. Fifty years ago, paper dollars had "PAYABLE IN SILVER TO THE BEARER ON DEMAND" printed on them, which meant you could take that paper dollar to the bank and trade it for a silver one. The government's promise seemed to be that for every paper dollar, there was a silver dollar to back it up. That message has a nice, confidence-inspiring sound to it, more solid than, "THIS NOTE IS LEGAL TENDER FOR ALL DEBTS, PUBLIC AND PRIVATE," the slim reassurance printed on dollars today.

Then again, silver is a valuable commodity on the world market today, which is a businesslike way of saying that there are places where people buy and sell silver and gold. Lots of it. And the prices change all the time, depending on how much of it there-is laying around at the moment and how badly people want it. If *supply* (how much of something there is) is greater than *demand* (how many people want it and how badly), prices for the something will fall. If lots of people want something (de-mand) and there isn't much of it around for some reason (short supply), prices will rise. This is the *Law of Supply and Demand,* the first great law of economics.

Suppose a shoe merchant buys a dozen shoes of a particular style from a manufacturer. The merchant wants to make a profit from selling the shoes, so she puts a price of $30.00 a pair on them. Immediately, customers start pouring into the store, buying these new shoes. "Aha!" she says to herself, "There's good *demand* for these things, so I bet I can *raise prices* on these shoes and they'll still sell! I can make more profit." See, she was the only merchant selling these particular shoes; *supply* was limited and *demand* was good—so the prices went *up.*

Now, the other shoe merchants weren't born yesterday. They see these new shoes whizzing out the door of their competitor's store, and they find out where they came from and they all buy several dozen pairs. "We're going to make a fortune," they say, but soon *everybody's* got these new shoes and the people who liked them most have already bought a pair. Suddenly, supply is up and demand is down. What will the merchants do? They mark down the price, hoping that if nobody wants the shoes at $30.00 a pair, maybe they'll sell at $20.00. Prices went *down.* This is the Law of Supply and Demand in practice. It works in the stock market, it works for kids selling lemonade on the street corner, and it works on the value of money itself.

So, people have wanted to believe that a dollar is worth what-ever stands behind it. In the end, the idea that a dollar is worth what stands behind it doesn't stand up, because the value of what supposedly stands behind it is *itself* constantly changing. Confusing, isn't it? Maybe the only sensible thing to say is that a dollar is worth not what stands behind it, but what people are willing to accept it is worth.

There is another way to answer the original question, "What's a dollar worth?"

The second way: "A dollar is worth whatever you can buy with it." Once upon a time, kids could go to the movies for a quarter. Now it can cost twenty times that. Clearly, from one point of view, the dollar was "worth more" then than it is now. We call the process by which it costs more and more dollars to buy the same thing *inflation.* On the other hand, when you could go to the movies for a quarter, working people used to make $15.00 a week. There were fewer dollars around. For a while (in the early 1930s), the American economy had far too few dollars around. Factories couldn't pay their workers and closed up; people lost their jobs and their homes. When there are far too few jobs and too little income, we say we have a *depression.* When we're partway to a depression but haven't got there yet, we are in a *recession.* So at different times in our history, the dollar has been strong . . . and sometimes weak.

You'd think a dollar is a dollar is a dollar, right? What could be simpler than that? It's not, though, as you can see. The study of how money works and how countries make, spend, and distribute money is the art and science of *economics.* Let's look at various kinds of national economies next.

Thinking About National Economic Systems

Just as we did with climate systems, we'll try to develop a system of descriptive names for the economies of countries. Remember our definition of *economics:* The way money is made and distributed. In describing countries, we'll ask first how they *make* their money, then we'll ask how they *distribute* it (who gets to have how much).

Don't get discouraged if everything doesn't come clear the first time. Something as complicated as economics takes discussions and questions and hard thinking. Remember too, there is little agreement in the world about economics. There have been wars over economic issues, and people within countries disagree bitterly about how the money is made and distributed. It's *money* after all—and the having of it or not having of it decides who gets to eat and who doesn't, whose kids get good educations and whose don't, who gets medical treatment when they're sick, and maybe who dies in bed. You know there are rich and poor families. So it is also with nations. Let's take a look.

Classifying Nations According to How They Make Their Money

Agricultural nations   Although there may be a modern city or two in agricultural nations, *most people farm for a living*. If the land is very poor, it may be *subsistence farming*—survival farming. If farmers need most of their harvests to feed their families, there will be little left over to sell . . . little cash to buy anything the family might need: books, clothing, medical care. If the population has little cash, there will be little tax money available to pay for national health care or other social programs. If the government just prints more paper money, the country will experience bad inflation and more problems.

Here's an irony (you might say an "irony" is the difference between what you've got and what you had expected): Many countries with agricultural economies receive aid from more developed countries. Often, this is military aid. Poor countries often use scarce funds to buy weapons. Even in famine-stricken countries, you will seldom see a hungry soldier.

We should not assume that all people living in agricultural countries are poor, uneducated, or unhappy. Farming is not only a business—it is a whole way of life, capable of offering deep satisfactions. It can be profitable, too. In some countries, a small number of families own almost all the land and peasants are permitted to farm the land only if they give up a portion of their crop to the owners. In such places, the unhappiness on the land has less to do with farming than with the way the land is owned and shared.

Resource-dependent nations   A number of countries around the world are very rich in one or two valuable natural resources, often oil. They have little else to sell, but there is so very much of what they do have that they can buy everything else they need. The governments in such places must be very careful. They don't want to sell too much too fast, and they don't want to sell when the world price for their resource is too low (here's another rule of economics: "Buy low, sell high"). They don't want to get into price wars with other countries selling the same resource, or none of them will make any profit.

Resource-dependent countries know that if their resource is *non-renewable* (something they can only dig up or pump out but once), then their prosperity will come to an end when the supply runs out—unless they *invest* their profits wisely. The oil-producing countries in the Middle East are faced with precisely these problems now, and that's why you'll find Arabians looking to invest in American businesses—or to buy out whole companies. They've not only got the money, they *have* to invest or face economic ruin when the oil runs out.

Developing nations   We refer to countries that are primarily agricultural but have begun to develop their own industries as *developing* countries. If they can succeed in developing their own industries, they can escape their dependence on the more industrial nations—stop the bleeding-out of their national wealth as they sell away their raw materials and then have to import expensive finished products from abroad.

Industrial nations   These nations have a wide range of manufacturing abilities. They have both heavy and light industry; they can make airplanes, cars, and ships—also computers, watches, and radios—and bombs, rockets, and advanced weapon systems. Industrial nations have much to sell. They also have developed *services*, which employ still more people.

In the future, some nations may offer primarily services to the other nations of the world: computing, information processing, designing, researching, and entertainment. In the service economies of the future, *education will be absolutely vital for economic advancement.* What is education, after all, but learning how to find information and do things with it? In its early days, the United States was a nation of farmers. (Now, the United States has more college professors than farmers.) From the mid-1800s to the mid-1900s, it was a nation of factory workers. From the 1960s on, more Americans have worked at information-processing jobs (sometimes called *white-collar* jobs) than in manufacturing jobs (sometimes called *blue-collar* jobs). These changes hurt people left behind by the economy, but they offer opportunities to young people in school who can train for tomorrow's jobs.

Naturally, in the real world, countries do not neatly fit into textbook categories; there are shades and combinations of everything we've talked about here. Still, these categories are useful points of reference for making sense out of the world. We've looked at how countries make their money, and now we'll look at how the money is *distributed*. The best way to do this is to think historically—to go way back in time . . .

Classifying Nations According to How They Distribute Their Money

Hunting and gathering   This is the oldest way humanity has made its living. It's natural—it's what wild creatures do . . . roam around a territory catching things to eat and gathering still more. It's a human pattern over a million years old, and for small bands with lots of room to move around in, the system actually works very well. There are places where hunting and gathering is still a way of life today. We can learn a lot from what remains of these people. Sadly, there aren't many survivors left; they've been visited to death.

Men do most of the hunting, but don't always catch something. Women spend their days caring for the children and combing the area looking for seeds, nuts, berries, fruits—anything (including insects) good to eat. The women usually account for 70 percent of what the family eats. If men are the meatwinners in hunting and gathering societies, women are the breadwinners. In many of the most primitive of these societies, women enjoy equal status with men and nobody is "wearing the pants" in the families. Pants haven't caught on.

Since the world's remaining hunting and gathering societies are living in the Stone Age, their possessions are few. What they own is easily carried in a bundle under their arm. These are not what you'd call *materialistic* societies; their possessions are replaceable. *Relationships between people* are far more important to them. Everybody depends on everybody else for survival.

Modern thinkers often think of this "natural" approach as an ideal state: no sexism . . . communal sharing of property . . . almost a complete absence of crime. Hunting and gathering as a way of life has proved a fragile thing. Few such societies remain, and the few left are either being hunted into extinction or are being lured into civilization by what appears to be an equally "natural" fascination with metal pots and pans, modern clothing, and transistor radios.

If, as some people believe, humanity had it made living in the natural state, why did we give it up? Maybe we were too successful for our own good; maybe there were eventually more people than the land could support and we couldn't simply move onto the land next door because other people were already there. Population explosions are serious. Either you find some way to limit your birth rate, or you find a way to increase your food supply. Failure to solve the problem means starvation.

Agrarian societies Perhaps under this kind of pressure, agriculture and the domestication of livestock developed. Maybe the discoveries just happened and we were led on by the pleasures and stimulation of living together in larger groups. In any case, the discovery of farming set off the *Agricultural Revolution*—and around 4000 B.C. almost everything about human life started changing.

There was more to eat, but nutrition was probably not as balanced as it had been when the diet was more varied and less starchy. Larger numbers of people crowded together in smaller spaces. The crowding plus the new diet saw plagues (mass diseases) stalk the land for the first time.

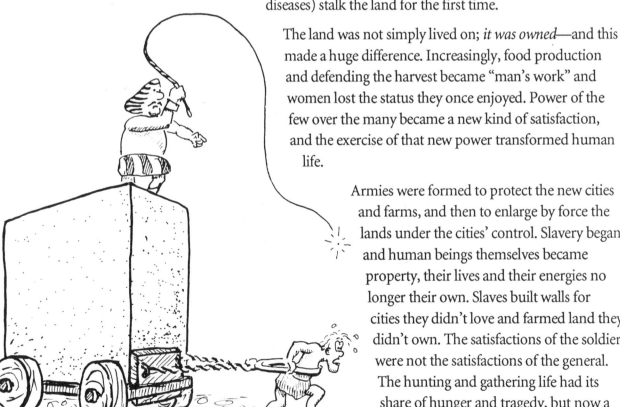

The land was not simply lived on; *it was owned*—and this made a huge difference. Increasingly, food production and defending the harvest became "man's work" and women lost the status they once enjoyed. Power of the few over the many became a new kind of satisfaction, and the exercise of that new power transformed human life.

Armies were formed to protect the new cities and farms, and then to enlarge by force the lands under the cities' control. Slavery began and human beings themselves became property, their lives and their energies no longer their own. Slaves built walls for cities they didn't love and farmed land they didn't own. The satisfactions of the soldier were not the satisfactions of the general. The hunting and gathering life had its share of hunger and tragedy, but now a new kind of suffering was born.

Also because of agriculture, much of what we value in civilization came to exist: large numbers of people brought more variety to human life, wider tastes, and more choices. Tradition lost some of its force and laws were developed to replace the stability people once had living as a part of nature. Art and writing assisted human memory and expanded the limits of imagination. Objects were created simply because they were beautiful, and those who could afford to collected them. Astronomy and medical knowledge was collected too, and with them, science was born.

As human numbers and tastes grew, so did a *material culture*—a culture that stressed ownership of land and possessions. Here is where economics comes in. At first, *barter trading* (swapping) was sufficient, but soon, real money was needed—and invented. Taxes were invented by rulers to force their subjects to pay for big projects. All these developments occurred within an astonishingly short time, historically speaking.

Feudalism   Usually, people think of feudalism as belonging to the Middle Ages (the period of European history from about A.D. 500 to 1450), when knights wore armor and lived in castles. In this book, we'll use *feudalism* to refer to how the money is distributed in an economic system: *In feudalism, wealth is based on the ownership of land by a few privileged families.* That's how it was in the Middle Ages, but that's how it's been throughout most of history. We need a name for that state of affairs and *feudalism* will do nicely.

Remember the few in feudalism. In Honduras in 1984, fewer than fifteen families owned 80 percent of the land. As of 1988, half of 1 percent of the population of Haiti owned 45 percent of the land.

Feudalism is an economic system in which the landowners *collect wealth* through rents and taxes while the poor get nowhere. Land is passed down through the wealthy families from generation to generation. In such countries, it is common to find military governments in power, supporting the right of the few to manage the nation's wealth and opportunities.

Capitalism Late in the Middle Ages, towns began to replace castles and their surrounding farms as population centers. Merchants and shopkeepers began to find new ways to make money through manufacturing and trade. This new wealth had little to do with land ownership. A new economy was developing: the capitalist economy. *Capitalism* is a system that *creates* and *distributes* wealth, instead of simply collecting it, as feudalism does. When the invention of the steam engine (in the early 1800s) made the development of heavy industry possible, the feudal landlords were the only people with the money necessary to build big factories . . . but they invested, hoping for faster profits. The Industrial Revolution had begun.

Capitalism offered far more economic opportunities to a much larger group than feudalism did. New ideas and new products stimulated new tastes, new demands . . . which in turn created more jobs for more people. The European discovery of the Americas and expeditions to the east brought in still more products and opened whole new markets—whole new groups of potential buyers.

The new age of capitalism brought with it new problems. Here are two. First, as the European countries founded *colonies* in the Americas, Africa, and in the East, a pattern started to develop. The colony would send *raw materials* to the home countries, and the home countries would send back *manufactured goods* to the people in the colonies. The home countries always made sure that they made more money selling the manufactured goods than the colonists made selling their raw materials.

This created a positive *balance of trade* for the home countries and a negative balance of trade for the colonies. *More wealth flowed out of the colonies than flowed in*—and often the money that flowed in fell into the pockets of a few ruling families. This too was advantageous to the colonial powers: prices for raw materials could be set lower if the income from their sale didn't have to be shared with all the people living in the colony. Capitalist nations began to like having feudal colonies.

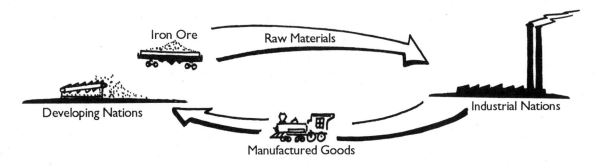

Furthermore, the home countries never wanted the colonies to develop their own manufacturing, because then the colonies could become economically independent and compete with the home countries—and that would never do. The colonial powers profited most from the system when they had all the advantages. Countries that were once colonies in the 1700s and 1800s often feel bitterness for the industrial nations. They often feel they were used—and often they are right. Do you see what's going on here? We talk about the way countries make their money (industrial . . . resource-dependent), but then we talk about how the money gets distributed, and the discussion gets really interesting. People argue a lot more about how money is distributed than about how it is made.

Here's the second problem in the history of capitalism. As capitalism grew in Europe and in the United States, new gaps began to open between the very rich (who owned the factories) and the very poor (who worked in them). In the early 1800s, there were no laws to protect children from being put to hard and dangerous work, and no protection for ordinary people from illness or injury. Factory workers often worked six days a week from five in the morning till ten at night.

A German historian and economist, Karl Marx, thought about the unhappiness of working people and wrote a book that eventually turned half the world upside down. The problem he put his finger on was this: Capitalism has the economic power to create comfort and security for everybody—*but will it?* How do you balance the desires of the few and the many? Capitalism has tried to lift the many; Marx wanted to start by eliminating the few. Historically, the flow of immigrants from Marxist to capitalist countries suggests that capitalism has brought happiness to the greater number.

Communism* or *Marxism   Karl Marx's book was called *The Manifesto of the Communist Party,* or simply *The Communist Manifesto.* Marx and others actually wrote many books on the subject of economics. In brief, Marx admired the lifestyle of the hunters and gatherers—especially their simplicity, generosity, and lack of possessions. He decided that *the ownership of private property was the root of most of humanity's sufferings,* and he proposed taking all of land holdings and factories from their owners and giving them out to the whole population to own and manage *in common*—hence the term *communism.*

Socialism   Marx did not imagine that if the rights of private property were taken away, whole populations would know automatically how to manage their affairs communally. He imagined that a period of adjustment would be needed. Marx imagined socialism as *government management of the economy.* In the former Soviet Union, the government managed the economy for generations, yet continued to insist that communism was its ultimate goal. Other nations, such as Sweden and Denmark, have no interest in communism—but they maintain mildly socialistic economies in which tax moneys finance free education and medical care. Most business remains in private hands. Well run, socialism can provide a comfortable life; badly run, socialist life can be drab and unpleasant. (For example, feudal Russia grew more tons of wheat in 1916 than did communist Russia in 1990.)

Back to the historical story. Writing over a hundred years ago, Marx figured that the lives of factory workers would continue to get worse and worse until they couldn't stand it any more—

at which point they would blow up and stage communist revolutions. Marx thought these blowups were bound to happen first in the most industrialized nations. Their workers would have lived under capitalism longest and would be the most fed up. By the time Marx died, most capitalist nations were afraid of the word *revolution*—even if their own government had been formed by one.

The industrial nations eventually had their revolutions—but not the ones Marx had imagined. They had *labor union* revolution. Workers gained (sometimes painfully) much higher wages and the right to strike (walk off the job) for more pay. Marx never imagined factory owners would permit unions, but they did. Ironically, fear of his ideas helped persuade many owners that unions were preferable to full-scale communist revolutions. Unexpectedly, the rise of labor unions released the full potential in capitalism. When workers had money in their pockets at last, they became *consumers*—they began buying things. Their demands created still more jobs . . . more people walking around with money in their pockets . . . and the whole capitalist system took off.

Most workers in the industrial nations haven't given communism a serious thought in over fifty years. Still, in one way, capitalism will always live in the shadow of Karl Marx. If the lives of ordinary working people ever slide down to the levels of misery Marx saw in his day, there will be the anger against the wealthy few that Marx predicted. We live fairly comfortably with great differences in wealth, as long as everyone has at least enough.

Marx's ideas have had the greatest power in the former colonies and the countries with feudal economies, where the lives of ordinary people have been most difficult. Marx wasn't an evil man; he just didn't understand the flow of history as well as he thought he did. Still, he was moved by the suffering of ordinary working people, and his message still has the greatest power in the places where ordinary working people are suffering most. A number of nations attempted to put Marx's ideas to work and created as much political suffering as any economic suffering they might have cured. In the end, they proved less successful in removing greed from economic life than in removing productivity. For the rest of *that* story, we'll have to look at politics—at the various kinds of governments in the world.

A Summary of Economic Language

In this chapter, we've looked at *economics,* the study of how wealth is made and distributed within nations and between nations. We've raised some of the problems associated with economics and developed a system of classifying nations according to their economic systems. This system works like this. We classify a country according to how it makes its money:

Agricultural   Most people farm.

Resource-dependent   One or two resources pay for everything.

Developing   On its way to an industrial economy.

Industrial   Most people have service and manufacturing jobs.

And according to how it distributes its money:

Hunting and gathering   Little wealth to own; cooperation is key.

Feudalism   Wealth based on ownership of land by a few.

Capitalism   Private ownership of wealth and the means to produce it.

Socialism   Government management of parts of the economy; tax-paid welfare.

Communism   In theory, community ownership and management of all property. When countries declare communism as their ultimate goal, we'll call them communist whether they have reached that goal yet or not.

With this approach, we can describe the economy of any country on Earth. The United States makes its money with an industrial economy and distributes it through a capitalistic system . . . therefore, it has an *industrial/capitalist* economy. Cuba's main exports are sugar and tobacco, and Cuba's government continues to distribute the nation's wealth communistically, so it has an *agricultural/communist* economy. People can argue about these things. Suppose Cuba's Minister of Information challenges this classification? "We are developing our industrial potential every day," she says. Maybe we're wrong, then. Maybe Cuba has a *developing/communist* economy. With a descriptive system like this, we can have intelligent and accurate conversations about economics.

As you read this, the last hunters and gatherers are disappearing from the face of the Earth. When they are all gone, we'll have lost our final touch with that ancient human voice that was ours before we became "Homo economicus"—economic man. The joys of possessions are many and varied. They include our love of the beautiful and of craftsmanship. They involve our work and extending our capacity to create and produce. Possessions also enhance our satisfactions of power and mastery over others, opening deep moral questions for us all. Soon, there will be no Stone Age advice to be had, but we can still read again the words of ancient philosophers and spiritual writers. As the Agricultural Revolution swept over them, they immediately asked all the necessary questions:

- How much is enough?

- How can love and justice balance the satisfactions of power over others?

- What is our obligation to those less fortunate than ourselves?

- How are the fruits of the land and the chance to harvest them to be shared among all the people?

Those are still the questions.

Project 9   *Locating the World's Economies*

After studying how the world makes its living, it makes sense to figure out which countries of the world have which kinds of economies. You can proceed by dividing the class up into continental task forces. One task force does Africa, one the Middle East, one Asia, and so on. Good sources of information will be encyclopedias (under the various continents) and some of the better world atlases. Also, world almanacs list this sort of information on a country-by-country basis.

- Where in the world will we find *agricultural* economies— countries where most people farm? You can look at this question a different way by searching for countries whose major exports are food products, as opposed to oil or manufactured products.

On the map, indicate areas with these codes:

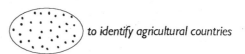 *to identify agricultural countries*

49

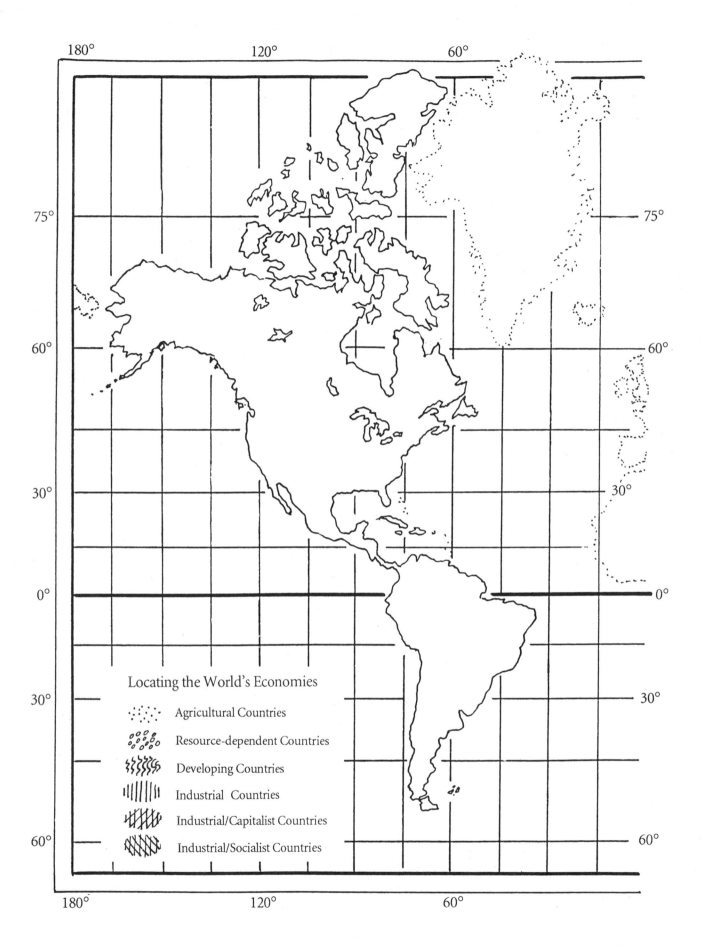

Locating the World's Economies

Agricultural Countries

Resource-dependent Countries

Developing Countries

Industrial Countries

Industrial/Capitalist Countries

Industrial/Socialist Countries

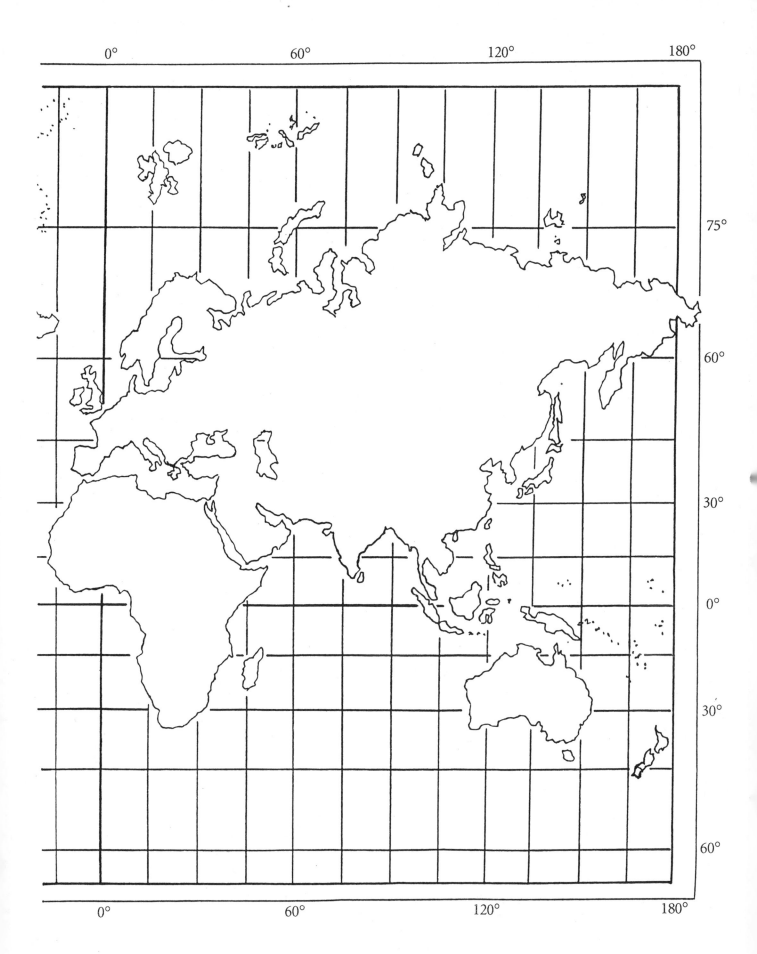

0° 60° 120° 180°

75°

60°

30°

0°

30°

60°

0° 60° 120° 180°

to identify resource-dependent countries

♦ Which countries in the world are the major producers of *oil?* We'd be especially interested in countries that are *resource-dependent*—those that have little to export but oil. Countries that have little to export but coffee or sugar, for example, and also resource-dependent, but might be harder for you to locate.

to identify developing countries

♦ Which countries in the world are *developing*—midway between agricultural and industrial?

to identify industrial countries

♦ Which countries in the world are *industrial,* where most people work in service or manufacturing jobs?

to identify industrial/capitalist countries

♦ If you want to get sophisticated, you can separate these into *industrial/capitalist* and *industrial/socialist* countries.

to identify industrial/socialist countries

When you're all done, share your information. Do you notice any geographical patterns? For example, are there differences between the countries north of the Equator and those south of it?

Chapter 5

The Political Earth

We can define *politics* as how power is held and used in public life. What is political power? *Power* is the ability to get other people to do what you want. While money is obviously a kind of power, in this chapter we're going to look at kinds of government. Governments use power in all of its forms. As our organized Alien has taught us, we're going to develop a political vocabulary, so we can talk intelligently about these things. Let's approach this by asking a question, then organizing the answer to it: *"By what authority do governments rule?"*

Monarchy   Kings and queens have the power because they inherited it.

Theocracy   In some countries, priests rule because they say God told them to.

Military Governments have power because they took it.

Democratic Governments have power because the people loaned it to them.

Please learn this before continuing.

Everything else we learn about these kinds of governments begins with these basic understandings. Naturally, it's not always this simple. Let's look at each of these forms of government in more detail, starting with monarchy.

Please learn this before continuing.

Thinking About Monarchy

Monarchy   Rule by kings, queens, princes, and so on, who pass the authority to rule down to their sons and daughters as an inheritance. A *monarch* is, then, a ruling king, queen, prince, or princess.

Royalty   The term we use to describe kings and queens. We use the term *royal* to describe the things they have and do.

Subjects   The people ruled by kings and queens.

Reign   The period of time a monarch rules.

Succession   The passing of power from one ruler to another. (This will turn out to be an important issue, as you'll see.)

Court   Refers both to the place where royalty does business (they "hold court") and to the people who surround royalty (the queen and her court). It does not refer, in this case, to a court of law where legal issues are tried, but it once did—when the king was the law all by himself and subjects were brought to him for judgment.

The Good News About Monarchy

Because power is passed down through the generations of a royal family, succession is not normally a problem. If it is, it amounts to a family squabble; the whole country isn't usually troubled by it. That's good news for the country with a stable monarchy. When there are no more royal children, succession can get very messy. Wars have been fought over who went next.

Because succession is not usually a problem, good royal families can devote their time and energy to ruling their countries . . . improving things . . . dealing with other governments.

Whether it's well done or not, monarchy is a simple form of government, easily understood by its subjects.

All this is the good news about monarchy.

The Bad News About Monarchy

The royal family may enjoy living well too much and put their personal desires above the needs of the country . . . spend money on things they shouldn't and tax their subjects for the money to do it. This has happened often. Bad news.

Monarchy . . . has the power because they inherited it.

While it may be reassuring for the subjects to adore their monarchs, the monarchs may begin to adore themselves too much. They may begin to believe that what's good for the royal family is good for the country as a whole. (The confusion between what's good for the government and what's good for the people is a continual tragedy in the world.) The royal family may be wrong here, *but who will dare tell them?*

If monarchs are powerful enough, they may make decisions on their own—even against the advice of their brightest advisers. Sometimes a bold stroke can work wonders . . . more often, decisions made against all advice do great harm.

Point: If King George of England had listened to his advisers, he might not have lost the Revolutionary War. There might not have *been* a war. We might still be part of a British Commonwealth of Nations.

Point: Inspired by the successes of the American Revolution, the French tired of their taxes and their high-living king and queen. They dragged the royal couple out of their palace in 1793 and cut off their heads.

Point: To live like a king is still the ambition of many of the world's rulers. (See Thinking About Military Governments, page 58.)

Monarchy Today

There was a time when most of the world was ruled by kings and queens. They usually said that God had given them the job. "The Divine Right of Kings," they called it. By claiming religious authority to rule, monarchs made any challenge to their right to rule a challenge to God's authority. It was easier for subject peoples to believe this when kings ruled always and everywhere.

Monarchies in most places collapsed when populations began to seriously question royalty's right to reign . . . and when people began to demand a stronger voice in government. Now only a few countries (mostly in Europe and the Middle East) have royal families. Even in these places, the actual decisions are often made democratically—by parliaments representing the whole people. Few absolute monarchies are left. Subjects can still love their monarchs and enjoy their royal ceremonies if they like (and they do—especially when the royal family has given up political power). The royal families assist their governments by taking care of ceremonial things: opening new airports, greeting visiting diplomats, that sort of thing.

Best of all, the royal families, usually well educated, can continue to think about the welfare of their countries and offer useful advice.

Thinking About Theocracy

Theocracy   The rule of a country or a people by their religious leaders.

Theology   Once called "the queen of the sciences," theology is the study of God and religious truth. Different cultures see their gods and their different gods' truths differently.

Scripture   A religion's holy books, in which religious history and beliefs are written.

Revelation   Normally, we learn about the world with our senses: sight, hearing, touch, smell, and taste. When people believe that their god has informed them *from inside their own heads* about religious matters, they feel they have been given a different kind of truth than they get from learning about the world through their senses. It makes their hair stand on end. People call *revelation* those things their god has revealed to them.

Because of the personal, inward nature of revelation, what is obvious to one group may be confusing or simply "wrong" to another. There is no scientific way to prove true the contents of human hearts . . . and because there is no proof, religious people often wind up fighting. It's ironic, isn't it.

Sacred   Refers to things valued because of their *religious* importance. Bibles, churches, synagogues, and certain religious rites are sacred.

Secular   A term usually used from a religious point of view to describe all of the things in life that are not religious. Using buildings for example, the Sistine Chapel (in the Vatican in Rome) is *sacred;* the World Trade Center (in New York City) is *secular.*

Theocracy . . . has the power because they say God told them to.

Persecution   Being made to suffer because of membership in an unpopular race, political party, or religion. A *martyr* is someone who becomes famous or respected after being persecuted to death.

Creeds   Statements of belief, usually recited during services of worship. *Dogma* is required belief—something people must accept to be members of a religious or political group. When we say people are *dogmatic,* we mean that they seem to insist that almost everything they say must be accepted without question.

Most people in the United States think of religion as only one element in their lives along with school, family, and work.

It is important to understand that not only does our culture (where and how we live) influence the details of our religions, it also influences *how we look at religion*—how important it is. In some other cultures—the Middle East, in particular—religion is taken much more seriously. Americans and most Westerners tend to think of life as mostly *secular* with some sacred things in it. Most of us would not be comfortable in a theocracy.

Some other cultures make sense out of the world like this:

Point 1: There is one God who made the Earth and everything in it.

Point 2: This God has set down strict rules for how every part of life should be lived—what we should do and how we should feel while doing it.

Therefore: The Western division of things into sacred and secular is wrong. *There are no secular things—everything is sacred!* Who is anyone to think he can speak for God, to say what things are or are not of interest to God?

Therefore: To run a theocracy, we don't need lawyers; we need *priests.*

The Good News About Theocracy

In a theocracy, you know exactly where you stand and what's what. The laws are clear and apt to be enforced to the letter. Everybody is expected to play by the same rules. No mid-life crises or adolescent problems "finding yourself"; the culture offers (and demands) clear life roles for fathers, mothers, daughters, and sons. If it's sometimes hard to live up to expectations, at least there is little confusion about what is expected. Having this kind of security can be very comforting—especially for people who feel their values or way of life are threatened.

The Bad News About Theocracy

Theocracy is often a response to a period of difficult changes. Rules in a theocracy can be so strict and unbending that the system cannot change with the times. (The leadership in a theocracy say the rules were given by God and therefore *shouldn't* change for the times or for anything.) People living under a theocracy may be unhappy with all of the strict rules and want more freedom. ("What good is 'freedom' when it only leaves people more room to sin," asks the theocracy. "We already know what we must do.")

Have you noticed something? The "bad news" is only our bad news. Most Americans couldn't live comfortably in a theocracy, but the system itself has answers to all of our objections. They're just not our answers.

Now you begin to see why political understandings in the Middle East are so hard to come by. We all see the world so differently.

Thinking About Military Government

There are many kinds of military governments, but they all have several things in common. Succession from ruler to ruler is not hereditary. When presented with serious problems, the military government's first thought is usually to solve them in a military way—with force or the threat of force. Military governments are usually not elected into power by their people, nor can people easily get a military government out of power once it's in place. There are many military governments in place around the world; they and democracies mostly share the planet. Some useful definitions:

Military governments (the generals, the dictator, the oligarchy) have the power because they took it.

Patriotism   Love of country.

Regime   Refers to a government in power. (The Marcos regime . . . Hitler's regime.)

Junta   [HOON-tuh] A Spanish term for a group of ruling generals.

Please learn this before continuing.

Dictatorship   Rule by an individual who has neither inherited power nor (usually) been elected. Dictators usually have almost personal control over both the military and the economy.

Oligarchy   Rule by a small group of powerful civilians (non-military citizens). The rulers of an oligarchy will use military force, if necessary, to stay in power.

Bureaucrats   People who make their living doing government jobs.

Coup d'état   [kood-ay-TAH] A sudden and usually violent overthrow of a government. Sometimes shortened to *coup*. It's French, meaning literally "a blow to the state."

Usurp   [yu-SURP] To grab power or position from someone else.

Civil rights   Basic privileges or freedoms assumed to belong to all citizens unless specifically taken away by a court of law. Examples are freedoms of speech, religion, travel, privacy, and a court trial if accused of a crime.

Plebiscite   [PLEB-uh-site] A public vote on an issue, or a vote to demonstrate public support in a place where the public normally doesn't get to vote.

Dissent   Public disagreement or protest. A *dissenter* is someone who publicly disagrees with official policy.

Here's how these words sound in proper use: "The *regime* of Marshal Strovos was toppled today in a violent *coup*. Power has been *usurped* by a *junta* of generals whose names have not yet been announced. Although the new junta has suspended *civil rights*, they promise to hold a *plebiscite* as soon as order has been restored to the country."

The Good News About Military Government

Often, military governments come to power when a nation is in the midst of a crisis, a war, a revolution, or an economic depression. Remember, the military is usually well organized. It has a "chain of command" to make decisions and carry them out. It has an organized system of communication. If the other systems of government break down, *the military have it all*—ready to go. The leaders in military governments usually love their countries. What could be a greater honor than "saving" their countries in their hour of need? Especially for the generals, it's what they've been trained to do.

The Bad News About Military Government

Military governments, whether generals in uniform or a group of bureaucrats in business suits, are convinced they know what's best. They think of ordinary citizens as soft . . . weak . . . uninformed . . . and they are ready to use violence against their own population to enforce their policies. They say they love their country, but that love is a very abstract thing. They don't seem to love their people much. In fact, the people are treated like pests. Citizens have no basic *civil rights* that cannot, in many cases, be taken away or ignored. We will define a military government by its willingness to cause its own population as much misery as would a conquering foreign army. In the name of "defense" a nation can wind up defeated by its own army.

The generals will look at the government and say: "What a mess we've become! The country is falling apart . . . thousands are out of work . . . there's rioting in the streets . . . rebels are in the hills and public morality is a disgrace. What this country needs

"Help! Police!"   "Police! Help!"

From Peretz as it appeared in World Press Review.

is a dose of boot-camp discipline: more organization, uniformity, respect for law and order . . . *patriotism!* Who is better trained in all of these qualities than the army? We're the only branch of society left who still know what we're doing and have the will to do it. *Let the army rule the country and we'll straighten the place out!*"

A dissenter to the military government will say: "The cure is worse than the disease! The military look down on civilian life as disorganized and trivial. In the name of discipline, they trample on the rights of the people, control or steal away our civil rights, silence our opinions, arrest, torture, and execute citizens without trials. They just disappear! Against the army's guns and tanks, the unarmed population is helpless. Sure it's nice to be protected from our 'enemies,' but who do you call when the criminals who assault you are the *police?*"

The problem of succession (the passing of power from one ruler to another): A military government has no "brakes"—nothing to stop it from going anywhere it wants. Only a very violent revolt can throw it out—and in the end, the generals are usually replaced by (you guessed it) other generals.

The dictator's spokespeople will say: "How fortunate we are in these difficult times to have our leader. History only produces such extraordinary men once in a thousand years, and we have one right here and now. The presence of such a godlike personality changes everything. In him lies our salvation and the answer to all of our questions. For God's sake, *give our leader the power and all your trust* to accomplish for the nation what only a genius can do. You can't be a patriot and turn your back on this opportunity."

A dissenter will look at the dictator and say: "You'd think nobody in the country had a brain in his head except 'our leader.' Putting everything into *his* hands scares me to death. What if he's wrong . . . who will tell him? Already he is eliminating every intelligent man and woman who doesn't flatter him with constant agreement. When the nation calls him the 'father of the country,' we all become like dependent children— helpless and dependent. Who can stop him now? All other branches of our government have been destroyed during our orgy of hero worship. True patriots love their countries more than they love their leaders. I say, throw him out *now,* if we still can."

Wide World Photos, Inc.

The Dictator. Adolf Hitler, 1889–1945

The problem of succession: The problem of succession is as difficult with dictators as it is with the generals. A nation accepts a dictator as an extraordinary human being—a savior. That is the explanation given to justify all the power given him. So how do you replace an "irreplaceable" person? The system has no answer.

Oligarchy: Rule by an Inner Circle

You might think of an oligarchy as the most mature form of military government. After all of the violent excesses of the generals and maybe a dictator, a nation gets tired. Things have to stabilize, settle down. If the government is not going to become more democratic, it must at least learn how to leave its citizens alone—at least some of the time. The terrors and the midnight arrests have to stop; the energy wasted on worry and passion have to be redirected towards getting the nation's work done. The government may still be military, but it must be more scientific, less emotional. It must wear a civilian face.

An oligarchy is a government run by a small inner circle of civilians. Usually these are bureaucrats (professional governmental managers), but at times, oligarchies have been run by the rich.

The members of an oligarchy will say: "Government is a vast and complicated business best left to the small number of dedicated public servants who have spent their lives doing this. We've worked our way up the long chain of command—we understand all of the subtle ins and outs. Unlike the governments run by dictators, we believe personality has little to do with it. It is competence and thoroughness—attention to detail—that count. Of course, we have the means to use force if we need to, but we prefer the quiet, unglamorous approach to get the job done. Slow and steady wins the race."

A dissenter to the oligarchy will say: "I don't know which is worse in the end, a government that breaks our spirits or one that *smothers* them. The bureaucrats keep us exhausted waiting in lines and wading through endless paperwork. There is a procedure for everything. Our leaders are faceless desk clerks picked from the Party's inner circle. They excite neither our loyalty nor our passion.

"And another thing: bureaucrats are, by nature, careful people, not risk-takers. They rise slowly to the top by making the fewest mistakes. Such conservative people can't provide the country with the bold leadership or the imagination we need now. I admit, it's better than in the old days, but I've learned the government can punish me for speaking out in a million ways without being so crude as having me shot.

"I guess I can live with it. I appreciate the stability. Still, there are times I find myself wondering why life has to be so *drab*. And I'm intelligent; why can't I be allowed to make my own choices? Sometimes, I feel as if all the nerves to my soul have died."

Project 10 | *Where in the World Is Freedom Under Fire?*

In this century, military regimes have brought terror and destruction to *millions* of the world's people. With your class, why not make a list on the chalkboard of all the times and places you can think of where it has taken wars and rebellions to defend freedom from military governments.

♦ Where in the world are people fighting for their freedom now? Where have people recently gained freedom?

♦ What kind of governments are in place in the countries you are looking at? What's the problem?

♦ What's actually happening? What news can you find?

Everybody will need a day or two to get some information together. Then as a class, collect the information orally and record your findings on the board.

Thinking About Democracy

You see the simplest form of democracy working in small groups. When something needs doing, people gather, and decide what to do and how to do it. Nobody is boss because the individuals in the group haven't given their power away, nor has anyone taken their power away from them. When the group reaches a decision, then the members *lend* out their power to support and carry the decision out. So where does the power in a democracy come from? *It comes from the people being governed.*

Democracy: the high-wire act

Many hunting and gathering peoples around the world—what's left of them—do things democratically because they live in small groups and the process seems easy for them. It doesn't even feel like government.

When what we call "history" got rolling, people organized in larger groups and strongmen took over . . . what we now call military governments. Then rulers wanted to pass power down to their children along with the family fortune, and monarchies got started. With few exceptions, kings ruled always, everywhere.

The ancient Greeks and then the Romans tried out democratic governments, but we won't go into that here except to say that our founding fathers in 1776 had the Roman *Republic* very much on their minds when they formed our government. Interestingly, their other role model was right under their noses: the Native Americans met in tribal councils to resolve important issues. The colonists were quite impressed.

The Basic Ideas of Democracy

When the *Declaration of Independence* was written (in 1776) declaring freedom for the United States from the rule of King George of England, it contained several radical ideas. Remember, at that time, kings had always ruled almost everywhere. The founders of our government said their political ideas were based on their *religious* understandings. They said:

1) It is obvious that since God loves everyone equally, then no one is "better" than anyone else. *All people* (including kings) *are equal.*

2) It is equally obvious that *God has given to all men and women* (the insight about women came later) *basic rights including life, liberty, and the chance to live happily.* These rights are not given to people by kings, but directly by God.

And here's the really radical idea:

3) *People form their own governments to protect their God-given rights.* The big idea here is that the people rule themselves; the power is theirs.

Starting with 1776, kings worried about revolutionaries and revolutionaries worried about kings. Here's a problem: The founding fathers knew that a government with strong powers was a threat to the freedom of ordinary people. *Governments and rulers always seem to want more power than they already have* (and more money, too). So they thought: *Government power is dangerous.*

They also knew that governments need power to get things done. You can't raise taxes, pass laws, or fight wars without power. So here's the other half of the problem: *Government power is necessary.*

There it is: central power is *necessary;* central power is *dangerous.* Such seeming contradictions that are nonetheless true are called *paradoxes.* Understand this paradox, and you understand democracy. Only democracy answers the question, "Who will rule?" with not a solution, but with a paradox. To the problem,

"Who will rule?" all other forms of government offer solutions: "The king will . . . the priests will . . . the generals will. . . ." Only democracy answers the question, "Who will rule?" by posing yet another question: "We need a strong government, but we're afraid it will steal away our civil rights." Here we have not a solution, but another kind of problem.

Problems have solutions; paradoxes have tensions. In a democracy, you have to keep your balance. Too little government power—nothing gets done. Too much governmental power—the people lose their civil rights and the horrors begin. Now you see why democracy is a high-wire act. Like the acrobat on the wire, a democratic government must do two things at once:

1) Keep its balance.

2) Make forward progress.

It has to maintain the tension—keep its balance—between too little and too much governmental power, and it has to get things done. To keep a democracy, people must design a complicated government where the responsibilities for different jobs are given to different branches. That way, no one part of the government can get too powerful and throw the system off balance.

Also, the people in a democracy must always pay attention and think hard. They have to protect their rights and tell their government what to do every time they vote. And they must vote! If the people don't use their power, the government might start making decisions on its own, and the people would lose control of their own future. As you can see, it's a lot of work.

The dictator of a military government might say: "Look, it's a jungle out there and our nation has to compete. Look at all the energy democracies spend keeping their balance and fussing about their precious 'rights.' If we took all the effort we spend on keeping our balance and used it for making forward progress, think where we'd be. We need to get stuff done around here with less talk and fewer delays. We can't afford democracy's wasted energy. *We'll* make the decisions around here and everybody else can get back to work."

It's happened before that a country has had a democratic revolution only to find itself—like the high-wire acrobat—so buffeted by problems and crosswinds that it spent *all* of its energy just trying to keep its balance. After a year or two of struggle for balance—and no progress—military governments have taken over in the name of "getting things done." Where in the world has this happened recently?

When the Constitutional Convention drew up the outlines for the United States government two hundred years ago, Benjamin Franklin stepped outdoors for a breath of air. A woman asked him, "So . . . do we have a king?"

"No, Madam," he said, "You have a republic—if you can keep it." But why do all the work? Why should any people go to all the trouble maintaining the tension between private and governmental power . . . keeping informed . . . watching out? Surely, there must be some reward that makes democracy worth all the trouble it takes—and there is: *freedom.*

Here's a difficult but useful definition of freedom: *Freedom* is diversity thriving in an atmosphere of tolerance. *Diversity* means variety. A free society lets people live in lots of different ways, doing their own thing—*thriving*. . . doing well—in an atmosphere of *tolerance*, in a community of people who mind their own business and let their neighbors be.

In a democracy, you find variety. It's interesting, exciting, and unpredictable. Citizens in a democracy can experiment, try things on, grow to become all they can be. No other system of government dares give its population this kind of freedom. That's why people who have become used to a democracy don't want to give it up and why people without one are often dying to get one. There's nothing like it.

Here's an irony: Military governments argue that they can move their countries faster by limiting freedom, *but the world's democracies enjoy the world's highest standards of living.* Why? Because in a population with lots of diversity—lots of variety—

people think up the most new ideas, invent the most new products, have the widest variety of tastes, and therefore buy the most stuff. Democracy is good for business.

You must have noticed by now that our explanation of democracy is much more difficult than the explanation of any other kind of government. There are two reasons for this:

1) Democracy—even understanding it—requires the most work from its citizens.

2) It's *our* system. Understand it or lose it.

That's why.

Project 11   *Is Your Family Registered to Vote?*

People in a democracy "lend" out their power to their governments every time they go to the polls to vote. Then the next time they go, they take back their political power for a minute . . . and then by casting their vote, they either give that power back to the same politician or give it to somebody else.

♦ See if everybody in your family who is old enough to vote is actually doing it. Bring the issue up at dinner. See if you can bring home some voter registration cards, if family members have not registered to vote yet.

♦ Then, talk about politics at home. Ask questions. Even if it's hard at first, try to get everybody involved. Become a politically active family.

♦ After making this effort, get together as a class and discuss how things went. Are families talking more? Were people already registered? Did unregistered members decide to get involved?

A Summary of Governments—The Author's Opinion

In this chapter, we've looked at forms of government, divided into four types: *monarchy, theocracy, military* (the generals, the dictator, the oligarchy), and *democracy*. We've introduced some vocabulary and reviewed the basic arguments for and against each type. Maybe we can most easily understand politics as a continual struggle between two basic human urges:

The will to power. This is the pleasure of exercising power over others and feeling superior to others. The urge to gain status and dominate others is almost universal in the animal world, as is the struggle for food. It has long been my suspicion that what is experienced in the animal world as necessity is, when satisfied, experienced in the human world as pleasure. We enjoy eating food and owning land and controlling territory; we enjoy exercising our personal power. For this reason, one of the basic human urges behind politics is the urge to dominate others and control their affairs. Here, you find one of the deepest satisfactions for those who rule.

The pursuit of happiness. This is the enjoyable opportunity to go on about our business without becoming the victims of people who want to enjoy overpowering us. It's also a basic natural urge to escape confinement, to search for food and company, to scratch where it itches, and to see what's on the other side of the hill. It's normal, in the pursuit of happiness, to want to avoid politics altogether. The only problem is that when too many ordinary people avoid politics, the game falls into the hands of the people who love power more than anything. And, *since power can only be enjoyed when it's used,* most rulers just can't stand leaving their subjects alone, but instead are continually experimenting with new confinements, rules to follow, causes and projects, and standards to conform to. Ordinary people are forced into politics to protect themselves from those who want the power to rule over them.

The important question for those whose pleasure is power is, *"How can I gain power over the mass of people and keep it?"*

The important question for those whose pleasure is freedom is, *"How can we organize a society that best guarantees the possibility of individual happiness?"*

When you observe the political goings-on in the world, you can see for yourself how the struggle plays out continually between those whose principal pleasure is the exercise of power and those who seek to preserve their own liberty.

"But surely," you argue, "there's more to it than this! *There is philosophy in politics, and belief in idealism, and the urge to create a better life—not only for ourselves, but for everybody!*" And this is so. But from time to time and from place to place, philosophies, beliefs, and ideals vary. They always have. The conflict between the hungers for power and freedom is always and everywhere. It will help you make sense out of what's going on in the world to remember first the basic human urges that compete for mastery in the political arena. Then listen to the speeches, read the words, consider the ideas, and make up your mind. Please forgive me if I sound cynical. I don't mean to be. I'm sharing with you what I think I've learned so far.

There is another issue to look at. *How do money and politics mix?* We'll take a look at what kinds of political systems seem to work in combination with certain economic systems.

If we asked the political philosopher how to best guarantee happiness, we'd hear plans about how to change the world. Our energy and attention would be directed outward into the world.

There is another kind of answer: to direct our energies inward into our minds and hearts—to change how we experience the world and how it makes us feel—to change who we are. These are spiritual answers. Those are the three basic ways we have for transforming our worlds into what we need or what we want: *economics, politics,* and *religion.* Now, a little political hardball.

Chapter 6

How Economics and Politics Mix

As you might expect, there is a strong connection between how a country makes and distributes its wealth and how it uses its power . . . between its economy and its politics. At the risk of oversimplifying things, here are a few patterns of income and power distribution:

Feudal/military   In a feudal economy, a few people control most of a nation's land and wealth. We can visualize this pattern as a pyramid with a tiny group of wealthy people at the top, supported by a huge base of poor folk. In such an arrangement, *most people are unhappy.* If these poor people could vote, the first thing they'd ask for is a different kind of economy—for a different system for making and distributing the nation's wealth. So a military government is usually in place in countries with feudal economies—to force the population to live under a system that makes them unhappy. The government serves the interests of a wealthy few. Democracy is not tolerated in places where there are gross inequalities of wealth and opportunity.

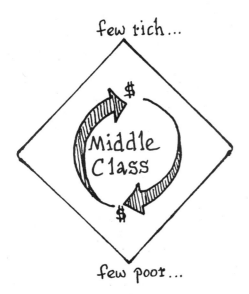

few rich...

Middle Class

few poor...

Capitalist/democratic We can visualize this system as a diamond. There are relatively few with tremendous wealth and relatively few who are desperately poor. Most people live in the broad middle class supporting themselves in laboring (blue collar) jobs or in management (white collar) jobs. They earn enough money to be active consumers of the products other workers make. Capitalism is an economic system that thrives on personal freedom—and the widest variety of work and purchasing choices. Since *most people live in reasonable comfort,* the government does not have to keep the system in shape by force. Participation is voluntary—so you'll usually see capitalism working in countries with democratic governments.

Capitalism under stress Before we move on to socialism, there is another shape we should inspect. The "hourglass" shape is a possible way to look at what happens to a capitalist economy when the middle class, the roomy center of "diamond" capitalism, is squeezed. The middle class can be squeezed by too many taxes, by loss of jobs, by reductions in pay, by rising prices, or by all of these headaches at once. In any case, when the squeeze is on, some people in the middle class do well and move up in income; others do worse and fall out of the middle class into the bottom of the economy. When this is happening, there can be more rich people, and more poor people, than there were before—both at the same time.

More rich

Middle Class Squeeze

More Poor

The middle class squeeze can be hard on democracy, too. With fewer and fewer people living in the center of the economy, compromises that please most people are harder and harder to find. More and more, what pleases the people on the top angers the people on the bottom, and vice versa. Politics get nastier. Democracy is under its greatest stress when large numbers of people are frightened or unhappy. If the people who benefitted most decided to use force to protect their advantages, you would find political conditions resembling the feudal/military triangle. So, there are political as well as economic reasons to keep capitalism diamond shaped, with lots of people doing well enough to participate not only as wage earners, but also as consumers.

Mild socialist/democratic Because capitalism works so well without government interference, there is always the chance that unfairness, greed, or bad luck will force people into poverty. As long as the numbers of poor are reasonably modest, the system has no problem with it. Capitalism can be heartless, even while it's being generous. There is a mild form of socialism that seeks to establish a "floor" below which no one in the population should be forced to sink. And where will the money come from to lift people out of poverty? Why, by more heavily taxing those at the very affluent top of the economy—the very rich. Obviously, it's *the government* that will have to do this, so we have *socialism:* government management of at least part of a nation's economy. As long as the system leaves a broad range of opportunity for the greatest number of its people, this approach can be popular. In Scandinavian countries, this system is supported by democratic governments. This income-distribution system looks like a stop sign. (The top and bottom points of the capitalist diamond have been removed.)

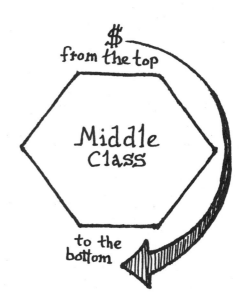

Communist/military In an extremely socialistic or communistic economy, the goal is to produce a society as close to "classless" as possible. This leaves the whole population living in almost the same economic condition. China came fairly close to doing this for a while, as did the former Soviet Union. History seems to suggest that this sort of life is very artificial. The population needs to be forced into this "pancake" structure or it will—of its own accord—start to spread out into some kind of diamond shape. *If force is needed to set up or maintain this system, we're apt to find military governments doing the forcing.*

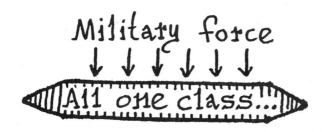

So there we have the basic patterns in which we'll find economic and political systems around the world. There are shades and varieties, of course, but if you can understand these, you'll have a better understanding of what's behind the news than most folks do.

Project 12 *Being the UN for a Day*

It's debating time. Maybe your class can be the United Nations for a day or so. Why not have each of you pick a country and represent its interests and opinions. You can find out about countries in the encyclopedia or the world almanac. If you know their economic/political system, you can make a fair guess about the positions "your" government might take. So study up. It's as much fun (more, sometimes) to be a villain as it is to be a nice guy. So prepare for a little theater. (Perhaps with costumes?)

Then, take several of the world's trouble-spots—the Middle East, Africa, the Balkans, anyplace there's real trouble—and ask the following questions for each:

- ◆ Who's having the problem?

- ◆ What seems to be their problem? Is it economic or political?

- ◆ What should be done to fix things up?
  Is this an economic or political solution?

You should have some good arguments, if everybody gets into it. Representatives of different countries, with different economic and political systems, won't agree on much. Will you ever agree? Become a United Nations and find out.

Project 13 The Starship Project

Many pages ago, we began this book with the idea of an Alien, visiting this planet from a far-off galaxy. Now it's time to turn that idea inside out. This time, we are going out on a space voyage into the unknown. How will we do this? You'll decide. It's your generation that will go.

Some things we know, and we'll list them now. We know that, though "warp speeds" make good science fiction, the technology available to us will give us speeds far below the speed of light. So first: *this voyage will take years,* more years than the span of an average life. The people who volunteer for such a trip must be willing to dedicate their whole lives to the effort. We already know from our current space program that people of such courage exist.

Well then, if the voyage will last longer than a single life span, then we also know that *children will be born in the Starship and will know no other home.* In other words, when the original crew volunteer for this mission, they will have volunteered their children—whether their children like it or not. Can't be helped, I guess. Then again, it's always like that: none of us volunteered either; we're just here.

If perhaps entire generations will be born and die in the Starship, then it can't just be a cabin made of plastic and steel. *People have to live in this thing happily—or they'll go crazy out there in the dark, far from home.*

This expedition is going to be like a dandelion seed, blown off into the cosmos by itself. If the Starship doesn't eventually find a fertile place to land, the trip will have been all for nothing. There's no reporting back to Earth after several generations. No radio signal could reach Earth, even if the crew knew exactly where to direct one—and besides, who knows whether anyone will have remembered to listen, or that listeners still exist. *Meanwhile, the Starship must be ecologically balanced.* Not only must it carry everything a star colony will need, it must continue to operate without running out of energy or filling up with garbage.

These things we know. Everything else must be decided by the group we have here. You are the corps of physicists, biologists, sociologists, psychologists, and astronomers selected to design the Starship and solve, in advance, all of its problems. Congratulations!

To get things started, we have decided in advance on the Starship's general dimensions. Imagine a field one-half mile on a side. Next, imagine rolling that square surface into a cylinder, with the liveable space on the inside. That's what we've got. We'll make the cylinder rotate to provide artificial gravity for those living inside.

We'll raise a number of problems next. In solving them, you'll be designing the Starship and making it come to life. In solving each of these problems, argue it out first, then bring things to a vote. Finally, record your agreements on the board.

- The Starship has a living area equivalent to a field 2500 feet (762 meters) on a side. How many people will be able to live on this thing for the long haul? What are the issues here?

- What will the inside look like? How will space in the Starship be used?

- What will people eat? What sorts of foods will there be and how will they be grown? (Why can't we just bring up loads of cans and frozen stuff?)

- We know the space in the Starship is limited. What sort of families should we have? What social needs do families meet? Will the space families resemble those on Earth, and how do you define a family anyway?

- The Pico family has just announced their plans to have a third child. Is that a problem? If it is, what sort of problem is it? This is going to be a touchy subject because of the strong issues of freedom and privacy it raises. What's at stake here? What happens to the mission if you fail to solve the problem?

- This one is related to the last problem, in a way. Grandmother Jones dies in her ninety-second year. What do you do with her body? What do you do with the remains of everything that dies? What are the issues here? What are the consequences of each choice you might make?

- Should there be school in the Starship? Or, to put it another way, what is important for everyone living on the Starship to know? Who will teach it?

- What sorts of professions should there be on the Starship? Assign every adult a profession.

- What sort of economic system should there be in the Starship? Should everyone be paid? Why or why not?

- What sort of government and laws should there be in the Starship? How do we enforce our decisions here?

Well, there you have it. Surely you can think of more questions, but this is enough to give you a fairly detailed picture of what kind of a Starship you think would work. Now, look at what you've done.

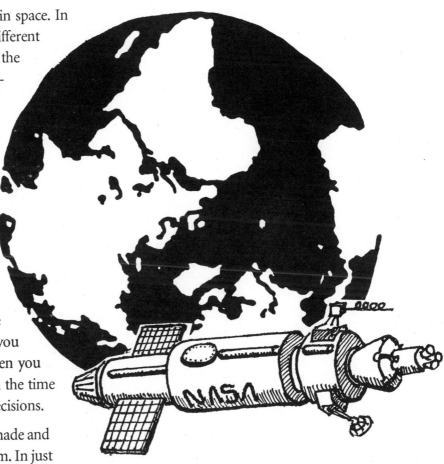

Here's your Starship, floating in space. In what way is your Starship different from the Earth itself? Surely the Earth is bigger and more complex, but aren't the issues the same, finally? Should you have everyone on the Starship the same race, for example? Aren't you asking the same questions people ask on Earth?

If I had asked you to redesign the Earth, you would have said it was too hard and complicated—but you did the same job with the Starship. If you say the Starship is smaller, then you simply knew for certain when the time had come to make the hard decisions.

Look at the decisions you've made and remember why you made them. In just this way has history brought you to the present moment.

Appendix: Maps for Your Own Projects

Use the maps on the next few pages to do projects on your own. You might want to locate physical features such as countries, major cities, rivers, or bodies of water; or other features such as major import or exports, types of political system or economy, or areas of current conflict. Be creative!

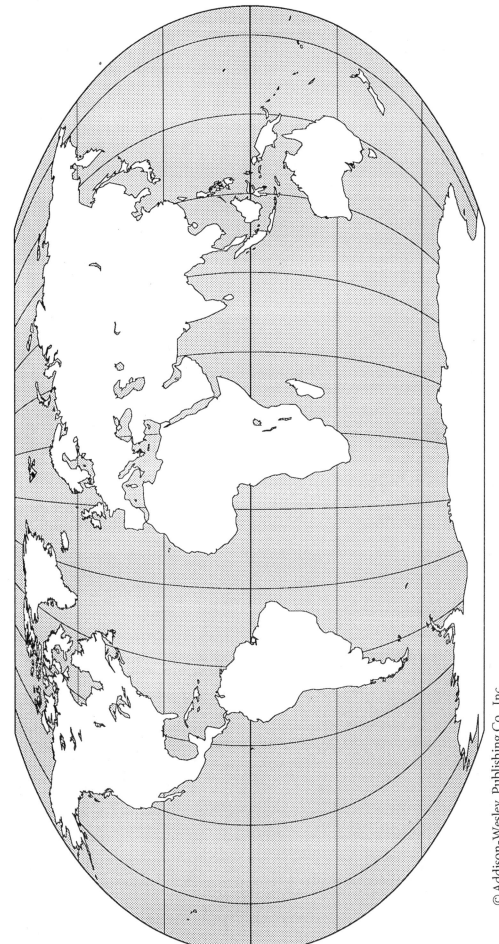

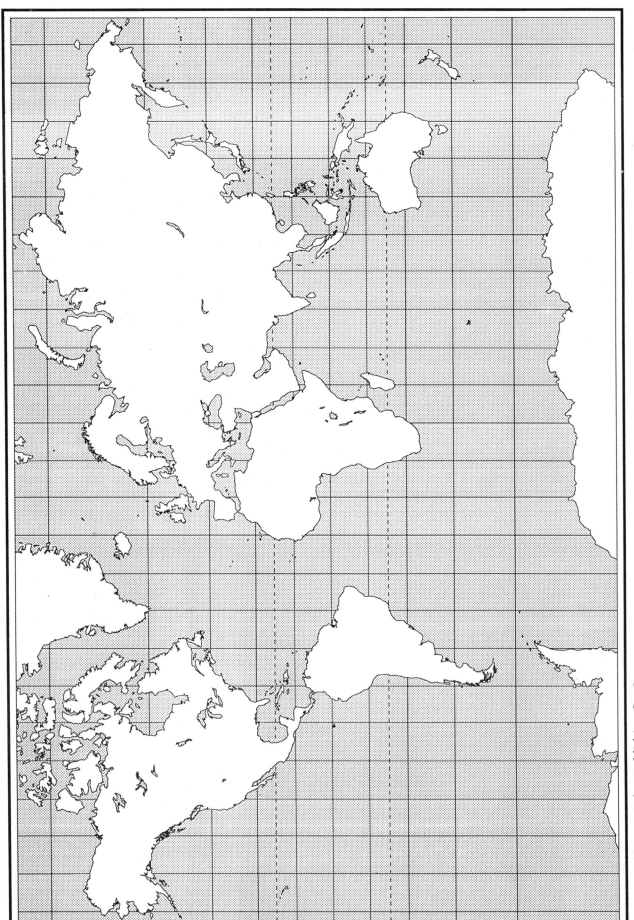

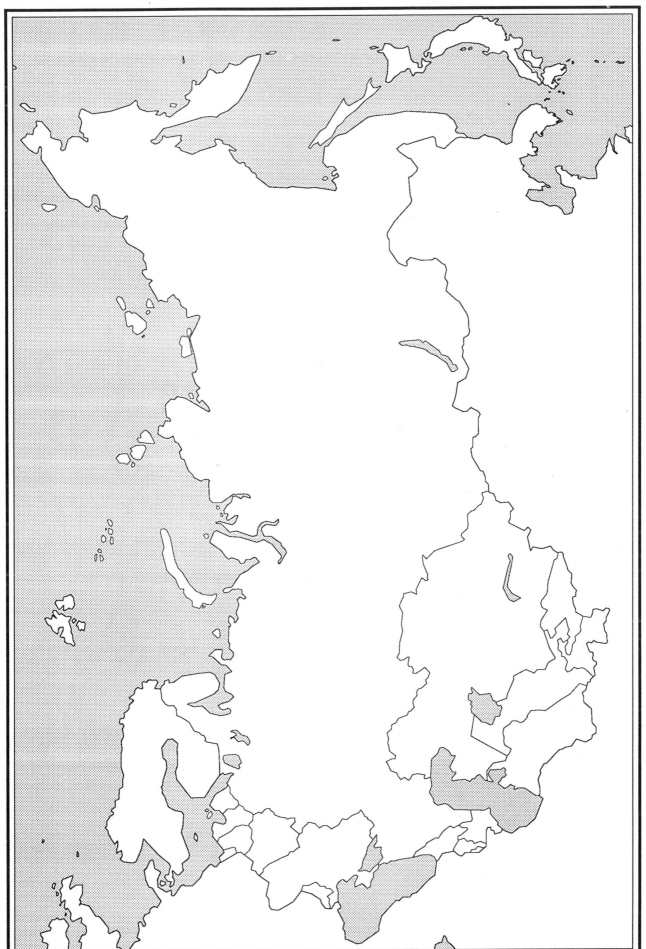

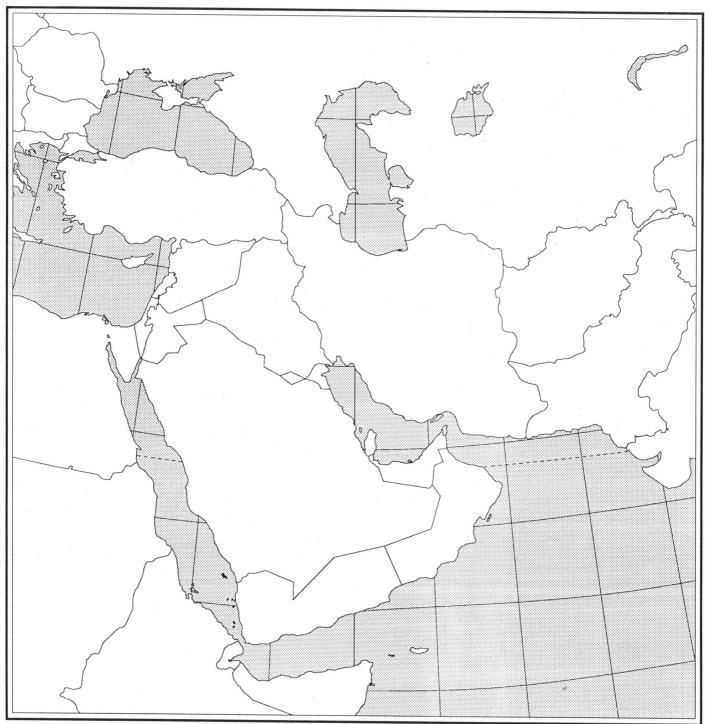

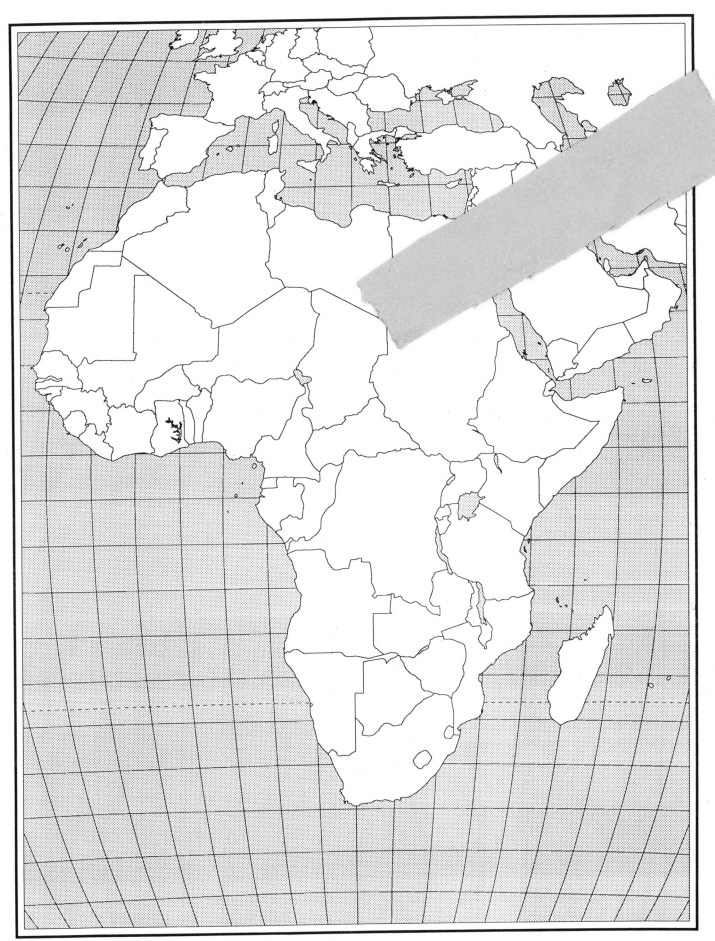

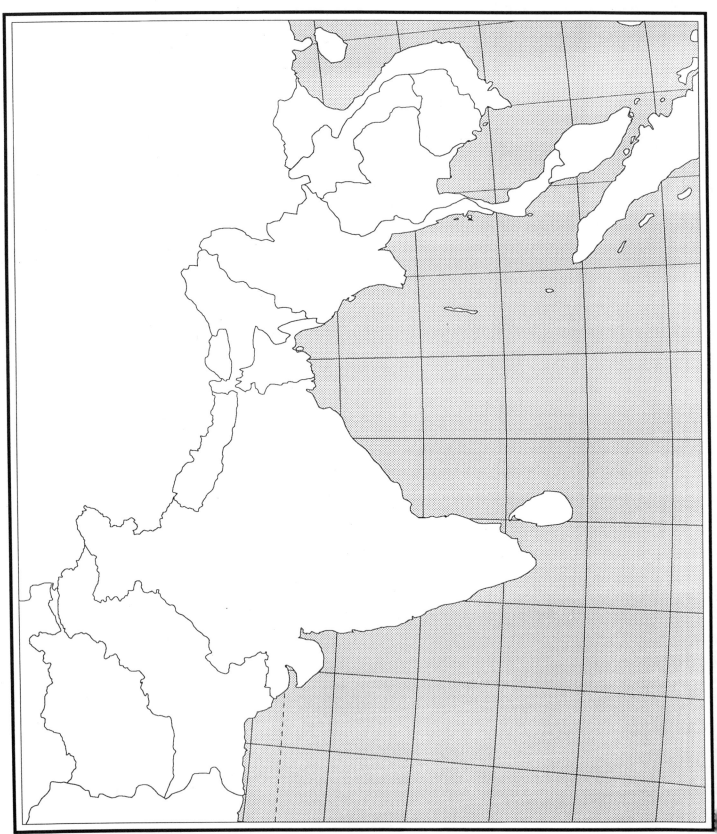

Index

Italicized numbers indicate definitions.

religious beliefs, 56–58

resource-dependent nations, *39, 48*

resources, non-renewable, 39–40

revelation, *56*

revolution, 47

rivers, 9–11

royalty, *54*

rural, *35*

sacred, *56, 57*

scripture, *56*

seas, 1-3

secular, *56, 57*

service, *34*

socialism, *46, 48,* 73

Soviet Union, 46, 73

subjects, *54*

subsistence farming, 39

suburban, *35*

succession, *54,* 61, 62

supply, 37

theocracy, *53,* 56–58

theology, *56*

tourism, *34*

transportation, *35*

tropical, *13*

United Nations, 74

urban, *35*

usurp, *59*

voting, 68

white-collar jobs, *40*